Top to bottom: Red-throated loon, black-footed albatross, herring gull and swan goose.

A pair of mandarin ducks.

Birds in China

Xu Weishu

FOREIGN LANGUAGES PRESS
BEIJING

First Edition   1989

Translation by: Zhou Lifang and Liu Bingwen
Illustrations by: Wang Binying

ISBN 7-119-00069-1
ISBN 0-8351-1967-X

Copyright 1989 by Foreign Languages Press, Beijing, China

Published by Foreign Languages Press
24 Baiwanzhu ang Road, Beijing, China

Printed by Foreign Languages Printing House
19 West Chegongzhuang Road, Beijing, China
Distributed by China International Book Trading Corporation
(Guoji Shudian), P.O. Box 399, Beijing, China

Printed in the People's Republic of China

Contents

Zhalong Nature Reserve in Heilongjiang Province.

Bird Island Reserve in Qinghai Province.

Introduction

China's earliest written records of man's observation of birds are etched on oracle bones dating from the Xia and Shang dynasties (about twenty-first century to eleventh century B.C.). The *Book of Songs*, compiled during the Spring and Autumn Period (770-476 B.C.), contains descriptions of thirty-five species of birds, a measure of the knowledge people had acquired about ornithology at the time. *Er Ya*, the oldest lexicon in China, compiled shortly after 206 B.C., describes the bird as an animal "with two feet and feathers" which is a precise scientific definition.

The bird was a special ramification of the reptile, and the two have many characteristics in common. Both lack sweat glands under the skin; the scales of the reptile and the feathers of the bird both result from cornification of the epidermis; both have a single occipital condyle connected to the spine; like the bird, the tortoise has a horny beak, and some reptiles (such as the chameleon) have air sacs linked to their lungs; both reptile and bird have hind kidneys; both are oviparous animals propagated through internal fertilization; the cleavage division in both is disc shaped; both generate serosa and amnion in the course of embryonic development, and both use the bladder as the respirator of the embryo. These characteristics are evidence of close similarity in the evolution of reptile and bird and explain why the bird has been described as a "prettified reptile." But an overall comparison of the two shows that the bird has many features indicating a more advanced stage of evolution and that it obviously represents a separate natural category in the evolution of vetebrates. Its having "two feet and feathers" is in itself a big difference from the reptile. Take the two feet, for instance. To be able to fly, the body of the bird underwent tremendous changes, the two forelimbs transforming into wings, leaving the hind limbs as the "two feet." The brain of the bird was also more developed than that of the reptile. This not only was important for directing flight but also raised the level of the organism as a whole. The fully developed heart of the bird ensured a supply of fresh blood for the whole organism, adding to its vitality. Next, the bird acquired feathers, a unique feature of this species. Feathers were the instrument for flying, and the long wing feathers supported the bird so that it would not fall from the sky. The tail feathers, also very long, played the part of a rudder. Other feathers, though fine, were closely arranged to keep the body warm. It is those feathers that enabled the bird to become a homoiothermal vertebrate, and the transition from poikilothermal to homoiothermal vertebrate represented a phenomenal leap in the evolution of animals. The body temperature of poikilothermal animals (such as fish, amphibians and reptiles) is directly affected by external temperature and rises or falls with the changes in atmospheric temperature, whereas the body temperature of homoiothermal animals remains at a relatively stable level without being affected by atmospheric temperature. This greatly strengthened the bird's initiative in adapting to the environment, extended its geographical distribution, raised its survival rate, and extricated it from the passive situation of the poikilothermal reptile, which is restricted to zones with a relatively mild climate. All these characteristics indicate that the bird is far more advanced than the reptile in evolution. They also constitute the major reason for the birds success in flying, seizing control of the skies and multiplying.

The shape and size of various species of birds can differ drastically from one another. Body length can vary from 65mm (flowerpecker) to 230mm (peafowl); the height from bill to foot can be as much as 3,000mm (ostrich) and even 4,000mm (the now extinct moa); the wing length can vary from 42mm (flowerpecker) to 850 mm (griffon vulture); the weight of the egg from 0.19g (hummingbird) to 1,000g (ostrich) or even 6,500g (the extinct Madagascar ostrich); and the body weight from 1.6g (hummingbird) to 144 kg (ostrich).

The habits and characteristics of birds are multifarious. They manifest special habits during the mating season and most species will find a suitable spot for nesting, hatching and raising the young. In the course of evolution birds have adapted themselves to strong environmental and seasonal changes. The most important aspect of such adaptation is their growth cycle (covering propagation, moulting and migration). After lengthy adaptation to seasonal patterns the bird's annual life cycle has become instinctive.

There are approximately 9,021 living species of birds in the world, of which 1,186, belonging to 80 families, are found in China, some of them rare. The rare endemic species are China's treasures. Of the 20 species of pheasants recognized as rare and needing protection, 13 are found only in China. Of the 56 species of pheasants in China 19 are distributed mainly or solely in China. The pheasant grouse (*Tetraophasis obscurus*) and eared pheasants (*Crossoptilon*) are among the special species. Species endemic to China include Chinese tragopan (*Tragopan temminckii*), Fukien tragopan (*Tragopan caboti*), Chinese monal (*Lophophorus lhuysii*), brown-eared pheasant (*Crossoptilon mantchuricum*), blue-eared pheasant (*Crossoptilon auritum*), white-eared pheasant (*Crossoptilon crossoptilon*), white-crowned long-tailed pheasant (*Syrmaticus reevesii*), white-necked long-tailed pheasant (*Syrmaticus ellioti*), Taiwan long-tailed pheasant (*Syrmaticus mikado*), golden pheasant, (*Chrysolophus pictus*), Chinese copper pheasant (*Chrysolophus amherstiae*), Chinese bamboo partridge (*Bambusicola thoracica*), Taiwan hill partridge (*Arborophila crudigularis*), Szechuan hill partridge (*Arborophila rufipectus*), white-browed hill partridge (*Arborophila gingica*), Hainan hill partridge (*Arborophila ardens*), and Taiwan blue pheasant (*Lophura swinhoei*). Of the 14 rare species of cranes in the world 9 are found in China. Numerous other birds, such as the natatorial mandarin duck (*Aix galericulata*) and swans (*Cygnus*), the wading birds crested ibis (*Nipponia nippon*) and little egret (*Egretta garzetta*), the birds of prey sea eagles (*Haliaeetus*), the terrestrial green peafowl (*Pavo muticus*), the great pied hornbill (*Buceros bicornis*), and the songbirds red-billed leiothrix (*Leiothrix lutea*), Hwamei (*Garrulax canorus*) and paradise flycatcher (*Terpsiphone paradisi*), are of similar value.

Some birds are of great economic value, for feathers, food and other uses. Pheasants and wild ducks are the main game birds in China, while the yellow-breasted bunting (*Emberiza aureola*) and sparrows are also hunted as game in southern China. Wild natatorial birds supply large quantities of down and colourful feathers for handicraft and ornament industries. Several species in China are major suppliers of guano. The Xisha Islands in the South China Sea, where boobies cluster, boast thick layers of guano accumulated over the centuries. Birds also provide ingredients for traditional Chinese medicine.

Birds contribute to the ecological balance in nature, bringing far greater benefit to mankind indirectly than directly. They check the overpropagation of insects, small rodents and other such animals, and some species, such the flowerpecker (*Dicaeum*) and sunbird (*Aethopyga*), which feed on nectar, help with pollination. Many birds of the bunting family, which eat weed seeds, help farming to some extent.

The government of the People's Republic of China has paid great attention to protection of rare birds since it was founded in 1949. A government directive calling for the protection and rational utilization of wild animals (including birds) was issued as early as 1962. The directive clearly defined the policy for intensifying protection of resources, taking active steps to domesticate and breed wild animals in custody, and hunting and utilizing wild animals within reasonable limits. This has been followed over the years by a series of related directives and regulations and promulgation of the Law of Environmental Protection and the Forestry Act as well as the Wildlife Law. More than twenty nature reserves have been established to protect rare birds. One is the Zhalong Reserve in Heilongjiang Province in northeast China, which is devoted to protection of the red-crowned crane and other water birds and of the wetland ecosystem there. The Bird Island nature reserve in Qinghai Province, northwest China, is responsible for protecting such water birds as the bar-headed goose (*Anser indicus*), brown-headed gull (*Larus brunnicephalus*), and common cormorant (*Phalacrocorax carbo*). Yangxian crested ibis reserve has been established in the Qinling Mountains, near Yangxian County, 107°40'E, 33°10'N, Shaanxi Province to protect the world's last known colony of the crested ibis, *Nipponia nippon*. For promotion of bird conservation in China, a Love-the-Birds Week has been observed since the Spring of 1982.

Chapter One
The Classification of Birds

Section I
Archaic Birds (Bird Fossils)

The first fossil specimen of the earliest bird — archaic Jurassic bird, *Archaeopteryx lithographica* — was discovered in the Solenhofen lithographic limestone in Bavaria, Germany, in 1861. The bird has now been determined scientifically to have lived in the late Jurassic period about one hundred forty million years ago. Sixteen years later (in 1877) a second specimen of the same kind of fossil was found near the spot where the first one was unearthed, and a third one was discovered in 1956. By now five such specimens have been brought to light. All the fossil specimens of the Jurassic bird have so far been discovered only in the same place in Germany and in the same geological stratum. None has yet been found elsewhere.

The oldest fossilized birds found in China date back to the Cenozoic era, during which birds became "modernized." They began to split and ramify at a high speed, forming many species and laying a foundation for modern birds with their great number of varieties and species, their wide differ-ences in shape and their extensive adaptability. The Cenozoic era, its tertiary period in particular, is important for the study of the evolution of birds.

Discovery of fossilized birds, particularly fossilized ostrich eggs in the loess of the Pleistocene epoch of the Quaternary period, has often been reported in north China and occasionally in south China. The ostrich, *Struthio camelus*, is a giant terrestrial bird that now lives mainly in warm zones. The African ostrich, the emu (*Dromiceius novaehollandiae*) and cassowary (*Casuarius casuarius*) of Australia, and the rhea (*Rhea americana*) are members of the ostrich family. Fossilized ostrich eggs have been found in China on many occasions. Fossils of not only eggs but leg bones have been unearthed in Zhoukoudian near Beijing, the site of Peking Man (*Sinanthropus pekinensis*). This shows that the climate of north China at that time was much warmer than it is now. The largest of all birds, the ostrich has long, thin legs, a long, slender neck and a small head. It is interesting to note that its head, neck and legs are all bare of feathers. Its feet have two white toes each. Its back is covered with feathers that do not form vanes for lack of barbules. So the ostrich cannot fly, though it has wings. Fortunately, it is fleet-footed, doing something like fifty to sixty kilometres per hour.

Ostriches live in flocks of forty to fifty birds each. The feathers of male and female ostriches are different in colour. The male bird is black except the head, wings and tail, and the female bird is greyish brown all over. Female ostriches lay eggs in the spring, each bird laying twelve to fourteen eggs in one season. They bury their eggs in holes dug in sand. Male birds share the duty of hatching. The eggs hatch in forty to fifty days. Ostriches are both herbivorous and carnivorous, feeding on leaves, grass, lizards and insects. The tale about the ostrich burying its head in sand when driven to the wall has been proved groundless in scientific research.

In addition, fossils of jay (*Garrulus glandarius*) eggs have been found in China's Inner Mongolian region, and fossils bearing imprints of feathers, possibly of the sparrow (*Passer domesticus*), have been found in oil shale in Qinghai Province. They date back to the Eocene epoch, about fifty million years ago. Of greater significance is the fossil of a bird named *Shandongornis shanwanensis*, found not long ago in diatomite in Linqu, Shandong Province. The skeleton is well preserved, about the size of a present-day pigeon but with a bigger head and a shorter, thicker tapering bill. Since its tarsometatarsus was longer, with the first toe not on the same plane as the other three, the ancient bird should belong to the pheasant family of the Galliformes. Three more fossil specimens — *Sinanas diatomas* (Anseriformes, Anatidae), *Linquonis giantis* (Galliformes, Phasianidae) and *Youngornis gracilis* (Gruiformes, Rallidae) — were later brought to light in the same location. The fossilized skeletons are fairly well preserved, except that the head and neck of the *Linquonis giantis* are missing. Such well-preserved bird fossils are not only the first of their kind found in China but rare anywhere else in the world. The *Sinanas diatomas* was about the size of the pres-

ent-day wild duck and was related to the ancestors of the wild duck. The imprint of its web is vaguely discernible. The hind limbs of the *Linquonis giantis* were thick and strong, similar to those of the present-day green peafowl, showing that it was a kind of large pheasant used to running on the ground. The *Youngornis gracilis* was about the size of a water rail, Rallidae. It is interesting that grains of sand can be seen in the hind part of the fossil skeleton. Since the base of the fossil is diatomite of fine texture, these grains of sand are conspicuous for their difference from the rest of the specimen, and because they are located where the bird's gizzard was, they could possibly be its gastric stones. Fossils containing gastric stones are very rare in the world.

The completeness of the imprint made by the skeleton of the *Shandongornis shanwanensis* indicates that the bird was buried on the spot where the fossil specimen was located and had not been moved over a great distance. Its spread wings and straight legs show that it was struggling desperately at the time of death. Analyses of the pollen in the rock containing the fossil indicate that a deciduous broadleaf forest consisting mainly of such angiospermous plants as elm, Chinese hackberry, walnut and beech trees was growing around Xiejiahe in Linqu, Shandong Province, at the time of the bird. The forest had underbrush and herbs. The climate was warm and humid. Near the forest there was a fairly big, quiet lake in which diatom was growing in great abundance. Twenty million years have elapsed since then, and phenomenal changes have taken place on earth. The forest around Xiejiahe is no more, the lake has risen to form a hill, the diatom in the lake has turned into diatomite. The bird fossil provides a clue to the history of these natural changes.

Many archaeological finds in China have birds as the main theme of their designs.

A fossil of *Sinanas diatomas*.

A fossil of *Youngornix gracilis*.

A fossil of *Sandongornis shanwanensis*.

Restored images of *Sandongornis shanwanensis*.

Apart from dragon and mythical *taotie* (a legendary ferocious animal) designs, many vessels from the Xia and Shang dynasties (2200-1100 B.C.) had phoenix and bird designs. The phoenix design of the time is now generally considered to be an exaggerated portrayal of the peafowl. The phoenix design on many bronze vessels of the late Shang period featured a crest and a long tail. A famous square teapot from the state of Zheng during the Spring and Autumn Period (770-475 B.C.) showed a crane standing among lotus flowers. Another teapot from this period bore the design of a wild goose standing guard over its flock at night. A bronze from the Western Han Dynasty (206 B.C.-A.D. 24) featured a flying swallow being trampled upon by a galloping horse. The Shang bronzes not only exhibit excellent casting, shape and design, but also reflect people's scientific knowledge of birds at the time. The owl design appeared on many food and wine vessels of the Shang period used by slaveowners for nocturnal revelry, vividly described in a poem in the *Book of Songs*. This shows that people in the Shang Dynasty knew quite well that the owl was active only at night.

Bird designs were also used to decorate buildings in ancient China. Eave tiles with twin-bird designs were found in the ruins of the lower capital of the state of Yan in the Warring States Period (475-221 B.C.) in Yi County, Hebei Province. Poems in the *Book of Songs* compare the eaves of palaces to the spreading wings of a pheasant. Many bronzes and carvings from the Qin and Han dynasties featured birds. The best-known include the bronze bird in the ancient palace of the Western Han Dynasty in Chang'an (now Xi'an) and the bronze bird cast towards the end of the Eastern Han Dynasty. An ancient square brick unearthed at Xidingjia in Sichuan Province portrayed an archer about to shoot at a flock of startled water birds. Bird designs are also seen in the decorations of the Ming Tombs in Beijing and Nanjing and in the bas-relief carvings in the Imperial Palace in the Chinese capital.

Section II

Natatories (Waterfowl and Others)

These birds, which live in the water, have webs that propel them forward. Their wide, flat bills make it easy for them to obtain food underwater. The diver (*Gavia*), grebe (*Podiceps*), petrel (*Oceanodroma*), pelican (*Pelecanus*), swan (*Cygnus*) and gull (*Larus*) all belong to this category.

There are three species of divers in China, which are by and large distributed along rivers or the seacoast in northeast China. They feed on fish, aquatic insects and frogs in rivers and shellfish, molluscs and other marine invertebrates in coastal waters. These birds dive into the water when startled, sometimes leaving only the head or bill above water. Divers usually lead a solitary existence, singly or in pairs. They nest close to water on islands or lakeside. Nest structure depends on location; nests built on marshland are generally composed of water weeds or rush. A female diver lays two eggs for each nesting. In the shape of an ellipse or a long oval, the eggs are olive brown or olive green with dark brown or black spots. Both male and female divers take part in hatching the eggs and nursing the young. Hatching takes about four weeks, and feathering some eight weeks. Though nidifugous, the fledglings often have to be carried on the backs of their parents to learn to swim and feed. Thanks to their large air sacs, divers can swim underwater a long time. They stake out territory during the breeding season. A female will occupy territory with a radius of two hundred to three hundred metres, while a male will extend it to five hundred to a thousand metres. Threatened by enemies, divers take to the water and swim away. Their main defence weapon is the bill, which they use to peck at the eyes of their natural enemies.

The grebe is a medium-sized natatorial bird and a good underwater swimmer. The species usually found in China is the little grebe (*Podiceps ruficollis*), which floats on the water like a bottle gourd and is therefore also known as the "water bottle gourd" in China. It has lobed webs and waterproof feathers soft as silk, and its tail is composed entirely of down feathers. Its body measures seventy to seventy-eight centimetres and weighs one hundred twenty to fifteen hundred grammes. Its toes have a one-centimetre-wide lobed web on each side and its middle claw has a comblike tip that can be used to clean the feathers. It is about the size of a pigeon, and its feathers are greyish brown. Little grebes live in rivers and lakes where there are abundant water weeds, which they use to build floating nests during the breeding season. The elliptical eggs are yellow. The female lays six to nine eggs each breeding season. Hatching takes eighteen to twenty-nine days, with both male and female helping with the brooding. When they leave their nests, grebes cover the eggs with down feathers or water weeds to keep them warm and protect them from their natural enemies. Grebes can swim underwater for thirty seconds at a stretch. The striped-back fledglings often swim under the aegis of their parents, which carry their young on their backs and flee underwater when threatened with danger, unlike the divers, which, their young on their backs, flee on the surface of the water. The little grebe is very sensitive and disappears into the water instantly when startled, but soon it reappears on the surface. The bird is extremely nimble and swift in diving, and even close observation fails to reveal how it does it. It does not often fly, because its wings are very short. When it does fly, it keeps to the surface of the water, its feet almost touching.

The great crested grebe (*Podiceps cristatus*) is about the size of a duck. It has a tuft on its head like the tip of a plait and a small ruff around its neck. Its wings are short and roundish and its legs, which are close to its tail, are good for swimming but not for walking. It often plunges its head into the water, then does a forward somersault and swims rapidly underwater before reemerging. The great crested grebe's nest, which is made of leaves of aquatic plants, is big and floats like a washbasin on the rising and falling water, thus posing no danger of drowning to the eggs or nestlings in it. The nest not only does not leak but provides heat for hatching through the fermentation of the water-plant leaves. The fledglings' downy feathers have several dark-brown stripes around the neck, and their colour is quite different from that of their parents. The parent birds together take care of their children and teach them to swim, first carrying them on their backs, then suddenly diving into the water, compelling the young to swim on their own and master the skill quickly. An interesting note is that grebes eat their own feathers and feed them to their young, the clusters of feathers and decomposed feathers in the stomach being helpful to digestion. Great crested grebes mate not only during the day but also on nights with hazy moonlight. The male and female court each other by a variety of gestures — shaking their heads, picking up reeds, tidying up their feathers and spreading their wings.

The albatross (*Diomedea*) is a large marine bird that frequents the China seas

Loon.

Great crested grebe.

Pelicans.

Red-footed booby.

Boobies.

Mute swans.

Mallards.

Bar-headed geese.

Common cormorants.

Peking ducks.

during the winter-spring period and is seen in Fujian and the Taiwan Straits all year round. It looks like the sea gull but is very stout, the largest being as long as one metre. The albatross are distinguished by the position of their tubular external nostrils, which lie at each side of the base of the bill rather than being fused on the top of the bill. Then nostrils are like pipes and their wings are long and tipped. The bird likes to fly freely and is able to stay motionless in midair for a long time, gliding on rising air currents, especially the unsteady air currents rising above the sea. Its long, narrow wings adapt to the changeable air currents over the sea and enable it to advance in the teeth of storms. Banding of a albatrosses has shown they can migrate over a distance of eight thousand kilometres, flying above or resting on the sea day in and day out except during the breeding season.

Albatrosses propagate on small secluded islands far away from land, and both male and female birds are responsible for hatching, which takes two to three months. Their nests are very primitive, often sited on low-lying land or in a heap of earth or grass. The eggs are white with red spots occasionally at the larger end. The young birds are abandoned by their parents immediately after being hatched and only after some time are they able to follow their parents in flights over the sea. Young albatrosses are capable of ejecting a kind of stomach oil when they are attacked by enemies. The oil is a pink substance secreted by the epithelial cells in the stomach and containing large amounts of glyceride and fats, representing undigested fats and remnants of food; it resembles whale oil when cooled. This substance can also be used to supplement the birds' preen gland in cleaning their feathers. Ejecting this substance can also reduce the birds' body weight, enabling them to fly faster to escape from their enemies. Moreover, the stomach oil can produce "physiological water" through decomposition and meet the albatross's need for water, since it has little access to fresh water.

China has two species of pelican, a large natatorial bird. It is known by several different names in China, including *taohe* (meaning river dredger) and *tang*'e (meaning pond goose, though it has nothing to do with the goose). The pelican is characterized by a complete web embracing the four toes of the foot, a powerful hooked beak, and a developed gular pouch suited to its habit of catching fish. A metre-long pelican weighs about ten kilogrammes. Its feathers are greyish-white and there are several black stripes on the wings. Its eyes are strangely small, in sharp contrast to its foot-long beak. The strangest feature is the huge pouch under its throat, which can be expanded or contracted freely like a fishing net. While fishing, four or five pelicans form a semicircle or line up in a row and, beating the water with their wings, drive the fish toward shallow shoals. Then they open their wide bills and scoop up the fish in big mouthfuls. By contracting the gular pouch, they squeeze out the water and swallow the fish. If they cannot eat the whole catch at one go, they keep the remainder in the pouch for later use. After eating their fill, pelicans open their mouths and dry the pouches by spreading them against their breasts. The pouch also helps lower body temperature during the warm season.

It is interesting that pelicans never change partners after the first mating. While selecting a male, the female performs a series of courting behaviour. The male, approaching his mate, often flaps his wings, performs a dance, and even makes a bow. He keeps brushing his beak against the female's feathers. After that, the two live together forever. A female pelican lays one to four eggs a year and hatches them by placing her feet on them. She scarcely ever goes away during hatching and resists the enemy with her sharp beak in case of an attack rather than abandon her eggs and flee. Both female and male hatch, and incubation takes about forty days. Then they nurse the young for another thirty-five days. Young pelicans just out of the egg are naked, blind, and dark grey, but soon a light, white down grows. The young birds depend entirely on their parents for food and protection. The parents first feed the young with half-digested fish; later they open their beaks and let the young birds pick small fresh fish from their gular pouches.

In flying, the pelican assumes a different posture from that of other birds, the head bending back slightly toward the shoulders and the neck twisting in the shape of an *S*. Since its bones and skin are filled with air, it flies adroitly despite its bulkiness. With just a few flaps of its wings it is able to glide quite a long distance.

There are two species of booby in China, whose habitat is the Xisha Islands in the South China Sea. The red-footed booby (*Sula sula*) is almost entirely white, with dark brown on its long wings. Hard and strong, its beak is more or less conical in shape, tapering off toward the tip and bending slightly downward, making it easy to catch fish. Red-footed boobies often live in large flocks and fish in high seas far off the land. They fly high in the sky, keeping a watchful eye on the sea below. When they spot a shoal of fish, they fold their wings and swoop down from a high altitude in a nosedive, then soar back into the sky with their catches, churning up sprays of water in a beautiful and fascinating spectacle. They are active mostly at dawn and dusk or on moonlit nights, resting or skimming over bushes and trees on islands during the day. Their heads sink into their shoulders when they are resting. Boobies play on rock beaches on windless days and, since their legs are short, swagger clumsily. On the larger Xisha Islands several hundred or even up to

a thousand red-footed boobies can be counted on each one hundred square metres. They sometimes fly into people's homes for shelter when they cannot find a natural refuge from typhoons.

Boobies continue living together during the breeding season. They build nests on rock beaches or in bushes or small trees, sometimes with four or five nests in a single tree. Some nests are just sixty centimetres aboveground, and some are on the ground. Simple and crude, the nests are made of a few twigs or blades of grass and seaweed. Both male and female construct, the male carrying the building materials and the female putting them together. A female booby generally lays one egg each time, occasionally two. Bluish-white, the shell is very rough, as if made of lime. The parent birds do not feed their young with fish but with cud from their gizzards. The thousands of boobies on the Xisha Islands have, over the ages, left a thick layer of guano. In the form of sand or rock, guano is an excellent fertilizer for its high phosphate content. The best-known guano producers in the world include Chile and Peru. In China it is found mainly on the Xisha Islands in the South China Sea.

The cormorant (*Phalacrocorax*), also known as the fish of prey, is divided into five species in China. Fishermen in southern China often use cormorants to help them fish. They tie the birds' necks with string to prevent them from swallowing the fish they catch. When their gular pouches are full of fish, they return to the fishing boats and the fishermen pick them up and empty their catches. In the case of a big fish two or three cormorants work together to carry it back to their master.

The cormorant is black all over, with a metallic sheen of bronze on shoulders and wings. At the time of breeding, some white feathers appear on the head and neck. The cormorant is often perched on a rock or tree in the water, waiting for food. It can dive to a depth of one to three metres, or even ten metres occasionally, and stay underwater thirty to forty-five seconds at a time. It often skims over the water, its neck and legs fully stretched like a wild duck. Cormorants breed on high cliffs or in tall trees. There are generally two or more nests, in some cases as many as twenty nests, in one tree. The nests are built of twigs, seaweed and motley grass and lined with fine grass. Each year cormorants return to breed in the same place and use their old nests. Nests on China's Qinghai Lake are all built on the basis of old nests, layer upon layer. Female cormorants begin breeding seventeen to twenty-one days after their nests are completed, laying three to six eggs each time. The eggs, in the shape of an elongated oval, with both ends almost equally big, are white with a bluish or greenish sheen. The male and female take turns hatching the eggs, and incubation takes about four weeks. Hatching begins immediately after the first egg is laid, so by the time the last nestling is hatched, the first young bird has grown to a fair size. The food provided by the parent birds is by and large monopolized by the first child, and latecomers are threatened with starvation. Both parents take part in feeding the young, opening their bills wide so the young can reach into their throats for half-digested fish.

The clustering of gulls often helps cormorants detect schools of fish. Once a school is spotted, it takes them just about half an hour to finish the hunt. The rest of the day is spent in cleaning feathers, courting and playing, or resting in trees to digest the food. When startled, cormorants will quickly take off and eject the cud to reduce their weight and escape from their enemy at top speed. After digesting their food, they throw up the indigestible fish bones and scales through a mucus sac. Gulls follow, picking up what the cormorants have discarded. Some people look on the cormorant as a major threat to fish breeding, but this view is not justified. Most of the food for cormorants consists of small, sick or weak fish of little economic value, and the amount they consume will be replaced by natural propagation. This, in turn, benefits regeneration of the fish population.

Nine different species of wild geese have been ascertained in China. Bigger than ducks, wild geese are excellent at both swimming and flying. With a flat body, assisted by a pair of webbed feet, they are like double-oared rowboats in the water. Native to Siberia or northeast China, where no insects, worms, seed or other food can be found in wintertime, they begin flying southward in flocks to warmer places in autumn. During the journey they act according to strict rules, with experienced old geese serving as guides in each flock, followed by the rest in a row or in a *V* formation, uttering the sound *yi-a, yi-a* while flying. They fly in a row or *V* formation because they have to make use of lifting air currents to conserve energy over the long journey, and the wings of the goose ahead create a slight upward air current for the one close behind. The lead goose, which does not enjoy the same advantage as those behind, shoulders the heaviest burden, so the geese take turns serving as flight leader. During the long journey wild geese often halt near lakes where fish, shrimp and weeds are available for food. Experienced geese stand guard while the rest of the flock relax. The sentinel on duty alerts the flock and leads it in flying away when danger approaches. It takes wild geese one or two months to reach a warm place in the south, and as soon as spring is round the corner, they fly back north.

Geese build their nests just before the breeding season sets in, but they are not very skilled builders. All they do is form a basinlike nest with reeds and water weeds and line it with soft feathers. A female goose lays seven or eight eggs each time and they are hatched in four to five weeks. Parent geese have to teach the nestlings how to swim and seek food. Young geese will be able to fly during the summer. Wild geese always return north for propagation because the summer days are long, food is abundant and the geese are relatively safe from enemies.

The domesticated goose came from the wild species. Many ornithologists hold that the goose was the first domesticated bird in the world. Some people believe the bird was first domesticated in Europe. Darwin quoted Homer to show that geese were raised domestically and used as sacrifices to Juno in the Temple of Jupiter as early as 388 B.C. Others think domestication originated in Egypt, because a fresco found there shows how geese were raised in that country as far back as 2000 B.C. Goose raising has a long history in China too. The burial articles found in the grave of a slaveowning aristocrat of the Shang Dynasty in the first half of the twelfth century B.C. include a jade carving of a domestic goose. Goose raising must have been very popular at the time if it was selected as the subject of a piece of art. The earliest record of goose raising among the people is found in *Zhuang Zi*, a book believed to have been written around 400 B.C., which contains summaries of the ancients' experiences in the form of fables. The chapter entitled "Mountains and Trees" has the phrase "ordering the lad to slaughter a goose and cook it." The above evidence shows that goose raising was very popular among Chinese at the time of ancient Greece and Rome, and the Chinese records actually predate reliable recordings in Europe and other parts of the world.

The largest bird of the goose family is the swan. Being rare, swans are under special protection in China. There are altogether five different species of swans in the world and three of them — mute swan (*Cygnus olor*), whooper swan (*Cygnus cygnus*) and whistling swan (*Cygnus columbianus*) — are known to exist in China. The black swan (*Cygnus stratus*) is indigenous to Australia, and the black-necked swan (*Cygnus melanocoryphus*) is found only in South America. The three in China are generally referred to as "white swans," because they are pure white. Their long, slender necks, full, rounded bodies, and leisurely way of swimming present to the Chinese the image of a tall dragon boat moving slowly forward. The mute swan, with its crimson bill and black knob on the forehead, is often compared to a fairy in white silk.

The bill of the swan is equipped with an abundance of tactile organs, including many Herbst's corpuscles, which are mainly distributed inside the tip of the bill. Along the upper fringe of the bill alone there are as many as twenty-seven such organs per square millimetre, as compared to twenty-three per square millimetre on fingers, which are the most sensitive part of the human body. Elegant in form, swans can maintain a perfect balance even when swimming in waves, because their legs and tarsometatarsi are short. Their feathers are coated with secretion from the preen gland to protect them from water. To reduce resistance in swimming, the swan closes the web and toes of the foot when it moves forward and extends them when it pushes the water backward.

Unlike the other species, the mute swan (*Cygnus olor*) does not have a circular windpipe, which is responsible for producing consonance, so its cry is husky and dull, hence its name. Cries are a signal of liaison between swans. They mate for life, the pair never parting. Mating is preceded by an "engagement" period. Swans meet in the autumn and choose their partners after displaying their beauty, but mating at this stage produces no result, since their gonads are not yet fully developed. The swan is an early maturing bird. Very young nestlings are able to swim, because their new feathers have been coated with fat from the belly of their mother. Swans occasionally carry their young on their backs when returning to the nests at dusk. Sited in reedy marshland or on lakes, swan nests are built of reed stalks and leaves, loosely stacked on the fringes and lined with fine twigs, reed leaves and down. The female lays six eggs each time and is responsible for hatching, while the male patrols the nest. In case of danger the swans quickly swim off, with the aid of both legs and wings, then slowly fly away.

Swans moult during the autumn, shedding all their quills for flying. Females moult before males whose quills grow at the same time as those of the young birds. Following moulting, swans fly in flocks to winter in the south. Some swans may cut their journey short and stop halfway when they find a quiet spot with plenty of water and weeds. Some swans fly over the world's highest peak — Mount Qomolangma (or Everest) — in their shuttles between north and south, setting the highest record in bird flight.

The bar-headed goose (*Anser indicus*) is a rare species often seen on China's Qinghai-Tibet Plateau. Small, greyish brown, this bird has two dark bands across its head. Bar-headed geese arrive in the highland lake area in western China as the weather is turning warmer. They migrate in flocks of twenty to thirty each, flying in a *V* formation at a high altitude and uttering loud, melodious cries. When they first arrive in the lake area, they stay in small flocks, resting on grassy banks or swimming in shallow water just after the thaw. The flocks gather for a few days on the ice, then disperse in pairs toward the islands. Bar-

headed geese build their nests close to each other, as many as fifteen nests in an area of fifty square metres. The nests are built in the shape of a plate just above the ground. The female lays two to eight eggs each time, in some cases as many as ten or even more. Incubation is the sole responsibility of the female and starts with the first egg. The male stands guard close by, sometimes tucking its head under its wing and perching on one leg. Bar-headed geese mainly live on grass and beans, but they also eat shellfish and other small animals. They may damage crops in areas where they spend the winter. Moulting begins in the latter half of July, when the geese lose the ability to fly and have to take shelter in secluded lake areas with plenty of water and weeds. They take to the lake and swim away when danger approaches. These wild geese are much sought after by zoos and museums because of their rarity and beauty.

Mandarin ducks (*Aix galericulata*) are the most famous of the thirty-three species in the duck family. Their characteristic of living in pairs is recorded in classical poems, the *Book of Songs* (*Shi Jing*) and *Book of Birds* (*Qin Jing*) compiled over two thousand years ago. One of the specially protected species in China, mandarin ducks inhabit a wide area in northeast China, covering the Usuli (Ussuri) and Heilong (Amur) river valleys and the upper reaches of the Tumen, Songhua (Songari) and Yalu rivers. In winter they migrate to southeast China and the lower reaches of the Yangtze River. The male duck has gorgeous feathers and a crest. A white band arches behind its eyes and light-brown fan-shaped feathers stand up on each wing. The female is greyish brown on the head and back, with neither crest nor standing feathers. They live in marshland, in broadleaf or coniferous and broadleaf mixed forests, on reed ponds or lakes, and occasionally in submerged grasslands or fields. They mix with large flocks of wild ducks in migrating during the spring and autumn. Moving to the Changbai Mountains in Jilin Province, northeast China, in April, they swim in the rivers during the day and rest under the willow trees by the riverside or in pits along the banks at night, tucking their heads under their wings. They build nests in tree holes high above the ground and place wood splinters and down in the holes. Egg laying begins toward the end of May, and by mid-June the parents take their young, half a dozen generally, to exercise under willow trees by the rivers. Shortly after the young birds are hatched, the male duck starts moulting and moves alone under the riverside willows.

The mallard (*Anas platyrhynchos*) is a large wild duck. The male is resplendant with bright-green head and neck and a white band separating the neck from the brown breast. The female's back is dark brown and its belly light brown. Mallards live in lakes and ponds with abundant aquatic plants and are seen in reservoirs, river bends and river mouths during wintertime. They stay the longest in southern China, being one of the main duck species wintering in that area. Except during the breeding season, they move in large flocks, each consisting of a hundred or even a thousand birds. Mallards are omnivorous, their food changing with location and season, including seeds, buds and leaves of wild plants, grain, algae, molluscs and insects. A female mallard lays about ten eggs each time, and the eggs are of two different colours, just like those of domestic ducks. Research shows that the domestic duck is actually a descendant of the mallard. Many different species of domestic duck have evolved in Jiangsu and other provinces south of the Yangtze River, where duck raising is popular, but their shape, colour and wings still bear much resemblance to their ancestor. The well-known Peking duck

evolved by domesticating the mallard and whitening its feathers over a long period. The appearance of the male bird and its curling central tail feather show that the Peking duck descended from the same ancestor as the domestic duck in the south. Signs of atavism are often seen on Peking duck farms, indicated by a few dark feathers or feathers in black-and-white check on a white duck and green-shelled eggs. They bear evidence to the fact that the ancestor of the Peking duck was not a white bird. Scholars abroad have maintained that domestic ducks were first raised in Egypt several centuries before Christ and duck raising was later taken to Greece. China may have started raising ducks even earlier than Egypt. The earliest written records of domestic ducks date back to the Warring States Period (475-221 B.C.), similar to the records found in Egypt. Since exchange between China and Egypt could not possibly have taken place at that time, the two countries must have developed their techniques independently.

Goosander (*Mergus merganser*) is a peculiar species in the duck family in terms of appearance. It has a streamlined body with a long conical or subcylindrical bill with sawteeth on its fringe. The female has a crest formed by feathers extending over the head and the nape of the neck. The male has a black head and back, white underparts and black scaly spots on both sides; the female has a dark-brown head, bluish-brown back and white underparts. The Chinese goosander, which is a rare bird peculiar to China, is limited in number and breeds only in a small area covering Hulun Buir League, the Lesser Hinggan Mountains and Lake Jingpo in western, northern and eastern Heilongjiang Province respectively and the Changbai Mountains in Jilin Province. Goosanders live in streams, river valleys, grassy marshland, ponds and wetland. Vigilant, they often stay quiet when startled, then quickly fly to shelter. They frequently move in threes or fives and enjoy diving. When they dive, they first rise up out of the water, then plunge down. They spend a long day, stirring at three o'clock in the morning and moving until dusk, when they return to their bivouacs. They fish in deep, slow water and lift their catches abovewater before swallowing them. After migrating to the Changbai Mountains in April, they begin looking for natural tree holes for building nests. Male goosanders often have false nests — holes where they stay for a little while but do not build permanent nests. Only in holes frequented by female goosanders do the male birds build nests. They also sometimes use old nests. Goosander eggs are long and light bluish grey with irregular rusty stains. Incubation, which is the female's sole responsibility, takes about one month. The nestlings are taken by their parents out of the tree holes to move around with other members of the same clan. Goosanders leave the Changbai Mountains and fly south in September or October.

Most gulls are marine birds, but a small number are seen over lakes and along rivers. Gulls are generally silvery grey, with webs between the three front toes. Their long tipped wings make them excellent fliers. They are precocious morphologically but late maturing in habits and characteristics; the nidicolous young have to be fed by their parents. There are thirty-two different species of gull in China.

Herring gull (*Larus argentatus*) is a large bird most often seen along China's seacoast but also found occasionally along inland rivers. It is snow white all over, with a sharp beak that displays a conglomeration of red, orange, black and yellow. Its wingspan measures three to four feet, making it the largest species of gull in China. A versatile bird, the gull can walk swiftly on sandy beaches, swim like a duck, fly at high speed or glide freely in the skies. A voracious fisher, the herring gull hovers over fishing grounds all day except for the noontime break, searching for fish with its sharp eyes. The moment a target presents itself, the gull swoops down like a bomber and cathches or pecks at the prey. If it misses the target, it plunges into the water in hot pursuit until the prey is caught. Though a good swimmer, the herring gull never swims long distances, only far enough to catch its prey. Flocks of herring gulls follow ships to hunt for fish or scavenge remnants of discarded food.

Herring gulls breed between April and August and build nests on seashores, islands or reefs, at lakeside or on rocky beaches. In the shape of shallow plates, the nests are built of algae, stems of water weeds, withered grass, shrub twigs, feathers and shells. The female lays two or three eggs each time, light brown, blue, green or grey. Despite its profuse feathers, the herring gull is extremely lean, because it is active all day and consumes a lot of energy.

Herring gulls sometimes can be very helpful to mankind by dint of their habits and characteristics. Sailors can detect the presence of reefs in the sea and avoid running on rocks by observing herring gulls and listening to their cries, because they often fly in flocks near reefs. Their habit of flying into and out of harbours often serves as a guide to sailors in heavy fog.

Section III

Grallatores (Wading Birds)

Wading birds live in marshlands or by rivers. With long, slender legs, long toes, and feathers only above the thighs, they walk easily in shallow water. Since their legs are long, they have to stoop low to pick up food from water, mud or ground.

This is why wading birds also have long necks. The red-crowned crane, black-necked crane, and white stork are some of the species in this category.

Egrets and storks are grallatores of large or medium size. They are different from cranes in that they live by water, their toes are thin and long, and the four toes are on the same plane. Both egrets and storks are common in China. They bear great resemblance in appearance, but the egret's middle claw has nodes on the inner side and its neck often bends like the letter *S*. There are twenty species of egrets in China and all are valuable birds. The white egrets — large (*Egretta alba*), intermediate (*Egretta intermedia*) and little (*Egretta garzetta*) — are very elegant birds. Slender and tall, they have milky white feathers all over. Loose straw feathers grow on their back and breast during the breeding season; those on the back are especially long and look like silk. Two long feathers behind the head resemble a pair of soft plaits that flutter in the wind and are very attractive. White egrets frequent rivers, lakes or paddies that abound in their favourite foods — fish, shrimp and frogs. Their legs, necks and beaks are very long, enabling them to get food in the water easily. In hunting, the egret walks slowly forward, its eyes glued on a fish swimming in the water, and suddenly extends its long neck and darts its beak into the water to pick the fish up. The egret's tail feathers are very short. While flying, it pulls back its neck between the shoulders, its big wings flap hurriedly, and its legs extend back in a very leisurely manner.

Egrets breed in the summer, when they build large, flat nests of branches and twigs high in the trees. The female lays three to six bluish-green eggs each time. They scarcely ever change the site of their nests. Each year they return to the old place to build nests and lay eggs, unless something unusual happens. The egret's white lanceolate feathers and straw feathers make expensive ornaments, much sought after in many countries. This has considerably reduced the egret population. It is therefore imperative to protect egrets.

The grey heron (*Ardea cinerea*) is the largest bird in the egret family. It has a white head and neck, with a black crest, mostly grey upperparts and white underparts. Grey herons are scattered almost all over China and are often seen in the south in winter. They gather in flocks of about twenty each, by the side of crop fields, lakes, ponds, on seashores or in shallow water in marshlands or grasslands. They sometimes stand motionlessly in the same spot for hours, drawing their necks back between the shoulders and waiting patiently for fish and frogs to appear. If startled, they throw up everything they have swallowed, then eat it all again when they quiet down. Grey herons tend to live together during the breeding season, with several nests built close to each other. There are one or two nests in each tall tree and occasionally a dozen nests can be found in a single tree, generally perched near the top, eight to thirty metres above the ground. Grey heron feathers, particularly those from the head, shoulders and breast, are of high economic value, but hunting should be restricted within reasonable limits to ensure regular propagation of these birds and a normal supply of feathers.

The stork (*Ciconia*) is a large wading bird. The white stork (*Ciconia ciconia*), which is found in northeast China, is a rare bird known throughout the world. Its beak is long and strong and its rear toes are well developed. Mild and vigilant, storks often gather in small flocks or wander alone in shallow ponds and marshes in flat country. They generally stand on one leg while resting. Storks are found only occasionally in woods or hills. Unlike cranes, they

Pratincoles (*above*) and great bustard.

Little egret (*left*) and grey heron.

Little egrets.

Grey heron chicks.

Purple heron in flight.

Crested ibis.

Red-crowned cranes.

Black-necked crane.

perch on thick boughs. They stretch their necks and legs while flying. They use thick branches to build nests in pine or oak trees and repair them each year so that in time they become huge structures. A female stork lays three to five white eggs each time.

The crested ibis (*Nipponia nippon*) looks white from a distance, but a shade of pink in the wing and the bright red of the head can be discerned at close range. Found only in China, Japan and a few other places, the beautiful and precious ibises are now very few in population number. They formerly migrated in the autumn to southern China, including Hainan Island, where they spent the winter, returning to the lower reaches of the Yangtze River, north and northeast China, or as far north as Siberia for breeding their young. They perched in tall trees and sought food in flooded farmland, marshland and mountain streams. The way they moved and looked for food in shallow water was close to that of egrets and they cried like crows. Their food included crabs, frogs, small fish, river snails, other molluscs and beetles. They were also seen foraging in paddies after the rice was cut. Ibises in Yangxian County, Shaanxi Province, northwest China, built nests in May in tall chestnut, poplar or pine trees. The female laid two or three light-green eggs with dull brown speckles. Nestlings were grey.

The ibis family, which boasts twenty-eight species worldwide, is scattered south of 45 degrees north latitude. China has six species, including the crested ibis, all rare and precious. Crested ibises are known to have existed in eastern China, the lower reaches of the Heilong River, Korea and Japan before the nineteenth century. Since they were unable to adapt themselves to the rapidly changing ecological environment brought about by human activities, this rare species is now on the verge of extinction. Only two crested ibises, all in zoos, are known to exist in Japan today.

Two crested-ibis nesting sites were discovered in 1981 in the Qinling Mountains at an altitude between 1,200 and 1,400 metres above sea level. These are the only flocks discovered in recent years.

The crane (*Grus*) is a wading bird of varying size. Wading birds are characterized by long beaks, necks and legs, with no or only slight webs. The four toes are not on the same plane, the hind toe being higher than the front toes. There are fourteen species of cranes in the world, nine of them found in China. Six of the nine reproduce in China. The Siberion crane (*Grus leucogeranus*) used to propagate in northeast China and is now returning in vast numbers; the sarus crane (*Grus antigone*) is seen only in southern Yunnan Province, and the sandhill crane (*Grus canadensis*) is only occasionally found in China.

The red-crowned crane (*Grus japonensis*) breeds in the Hulun Buir League in Inner Mongolia, Qiqihar and the central part of the Heilong-Songhua-Nenjiang Plain in Heilongjiang Province, and the Baicheng area of Jilin Province. It migrates through the northern coastal provinces down to the lower reaches of the Yangtze River and southeast China, where it spends the winter. China has built a nature reserve to protect cranes in the Zhalong area near Qiqihar in Heilongjiang.

The red-crowned crane's feathers are almost entirely white, with only part of the secondaries and tertiaries in the wings black. Its head is bare except for the red crown, which gives the bird its name. Red-crowned cranes used to be so rare that people seldom saw them, but the good work of the Zhalong Nature Reserve is increasing their numbers. While flying, red-crowned cranes extend their necks and legs in a very elegant style. Ancient Chinese imagined them to be the companions of celestial beings or described them as their carriers, hence called them celestial cranes. Chinese tradition regards the crane as a symbol of longevity, just like the pine tree among plants, and in traditional paintings the crane and the pine are often painted together to symbolize long life. In reality, the crane, which lives in marshlands, has very little to do with the pine. It often stands still for a long time, only stretching its neck to look into the distance. Its cries are very loud and resonant, because its long windpipe bends like a trumpet in front of its breast. A poem in the *Book of Songs* (*Shi Jing*) claims its cries can reach heaven. Red-crowned cranes breed between April and June, when they build nests on low-lying, wet ground. Large, flat, with a slight depression in the middle, the nests are almost entirely reed or cattail. The eggs look like duck eggs; their shells are light olive-brown with reddish-brown, bluish-grey or greyish-purple spots on them. Both male and female take part in hatching, with the female brooding during the day and the male during the night. The nestlings can walk unsteadily the moment they are hatched, but they still need parental care.

The red-crowned crane is a mild bird that lives on simple food, enjoys a long life and is easy to keep. Crane raising became popular in China as early as the Eastern Zhou Dynasty (770-475 B.C.). Rulers of some of the principalities at the time were almost addicted to it. Cranes were also trained to perform dances in the imperial court and entertain the royal family and nobility in ancient China.

The black-necked crane (*Grus nigricollis*) is the only high-altitude species in the crane family. It multiplies in mountain swamps 3,500 to 5,000 metres above sea level. It was first discovered in 1876, the last species of crane to be identified. In China black-necked cranes live on islands in highland lakes in Qinghai and western Sichuan provinces and migrate through the Qinghai-Tibet Plateau to winter in southwestern Sichuan, western Guizhou, and southern Yunnan and Tibet, or even farther south. They have been seen in flocks of three hundred to five hundred each at the Tangla Mountain pass and the Qaidam Basin in Qinghai while on their way south. Though relatively rare, black-necked cranes still remain in some numbers, probably because they have been free from indiscriminate hunting.

The great bustard (*Otis tarda*) lives on expansive grasslands or sandy land. It is tall and has a broad back, weighing six or seven kilograms. Its small head with flat bill is perched on a short neck. Its legs are bare and long, with only three toes on each foot. It runs so fast that it can easily overtake a cantering horse. The vast, empty grasslands of Inner Mongolia enable great bustards to detect any approaching danger. Well before the enemy or danger is anywhere near them, they begin to run against the wind and then, flapping their wings slowly but fully, fly smoothly at a low height and disappear into the distance. They feed on fresh green grass, clenching the blades of grass in their flat bills, raising their heads to break the grass, then swallowing down the whole lot. During the breeding season they like to eat tender grass and insects, their favourite being locusts. They begin breeding the young in late spring and early summer, when they build simple, crude nests on high, dry grassy mounds. The female lays two or three eggs each time. The male and female take turns brooding, and since they are very similar in appearance, many people used to think that all bustards were female. Bustards are first-rate game, their meat being very delicious, and bustard feathers are a favourite ornament for women's hats in Europe. Excessive hunting has greatly depleted the bustard population and the bird became extinct in England back in 1838.

Steps should be taken to protect this rare bird and to utilize this natural resource rationally.

The plover (*Charadrius*) and the sandpiper (*Tringa*) are wading birds of medium and small sizes. They fall into many different subspecies, widely distributed over the northern hemisphere. Their feathers are by and large sandy in colour. Their tipped wings make them excellent runners as well as flyers. The colour of their feathers helps them hide from danger, and they can take off abruptly and fly in any direction. The parent birds often resort to "diverting tactics" to protect their young from danger. A favourite tactic is to pretend to be injured, dragging one wing, so that the enemy chases them and leaves their young alone. The green sandpiper (*Tringa ochropus*) is the most common species in the sandpiper family. It is the bird referred to in the old Chinese saying, "When the snipe and the clam grapple, the fisherman profits." Green sandpipers live along seacoasts or in marshland, ponds or river deltas. They move singly in most cases, but when the nestlings are growing, old and young often stay together in flocks of several dozen to a hundred. They often perch on top of rocks by the seaside and wait for the tide to ebb so they can hunt for food in silt or sand. If their beaks cannot reach to a sufficient depth, they jump up and use the weight of the whole body to help thrust the beak deeper into the sand. They fly away immediately when people approach them. They build nests in well-sheltered places, using stems and blades of grass to form a structure in the shape of a shallow plate, which, strictly speaking, cannot be called a nest. The female lays three to five or six to eight eggs each time, and the male and female take turns brooding. When enemies approach the nest, the parent birds fly away and hover in the sky, crying incessantly.

The eastern golden plover (*Pluvialis dominica*) is also known as the "golden back." The male is black with golden speckles all over the upperparts. A long, broad stripe extends from its forehead down both sides of the neck and breast. There are white speckles on the underparts of the female, which lays eggs on floodland. The eggs are in the shape of a pear and of a colour very similar to that of the surrounding sand and stone, which makes them hard to see even at close range. Eastern golden plovers fly swiftly and land in a spiral. While flying at a high altitude, they utter loud, melodious cries that can often be heard in the morning and evening. They also hold the record for nonstop flying among all birds. One species, which breeds on the west coast of Alaska or in northeast Siberia, migrates south along the Chinese coast or flies over the Pacific for four thousand kilometres to Hawaii and farther south to its wintering site.

The eastern collared pratincole (*Glareola maldivarum*), a ploverlike bird, is greyish brown above, with a brown breast, white rump and chestnut axillaries. The species found in China is an able killer of locusts. Surveys in the Weishan Lake area of Shandong Province showed a nestful of these pratincoles could wipe out 162,000 locusts in a month. They fly fast, but only for two to three hundred metres at a stretch, and land very fast too, sometimes almost vertically. During the breeding season in summer they often gather in flocks of varying sizes, the largest consisting of as many as a hundred birds, and fly in a semicircle. They search for food in the air or on the ground. Hunting on the ground, pratincoles often make a short dash, switching direction from time to time. They fly like swallows, run like plovers, and lay eggs in dirt. They migrate to the Weishan Lake area in April, when they feed mainly on beetles and stinkbugs. Then they switch to locusts in June, when these insects begin to grow in large numbers. Pratincoles stay in Shandong for at least four months, during which they breed and nurse their young. It is in this period that each nestful of pratincoles consumes an average of 65,000 locusts, playing a useful role as a natural enemy of locusts, which ravage farm crops.

Section IV

Gallinae (Game Birds)

Most birds of the order Galliformes are residents. They are generally of strong build, with strong beaks, legs and hooked claws capable of digging. The cock and the hen vary in colour and build.

Pheasants follow complicated courting behaviour and are belligerent during breeding.

China boasts fifty-six species of pheasants, accounting for one fifth of the world's total. They are prized for their meat and plumage and some are sought after as ornamental birds. Quite a number of pheasant species are rare birds endemic to China, such as the golden pheasant (*Chrysolophus pictus*), Chinese copper pheasant (*C. amherstiae*), eared pheasants (*Crossoptilon*), tragopans (*Tragopan*), Chinese monal (*Lophophorus lhuysii*) and green peafowl (*Pavo muticus*).

The small-billed capercaillie (*Tetrao urogallus*), the hazel grouse (*Bonasia bonasia*) and the willow ptarmigan (*Lagopus lagopus*) are representative of species native to the northernmost part of northeast China. Their tarsi are feathered and their legs are without spurs, all different from their cousins. The small-billed pheasants, also called *feilong*, or "flying dragon," reside in damp marshes of pine and spruce forests, living partly in trees and partly on the ground. They feed on a wide variety of tree leaves, strawberries and moss, but the young depend entirely on insects fed them by their parents. The hardest time for the capercaillies is the snowbound months, when everything high in the mountains is under a blanket of snow. In those months they are forced to fly to the valleys or near the foot of mountains in groups. The cock stands triumphantly on top of a rise in a clearing while the hen squats nearby. If another cock draws near, a fight instantly flares up. The fighting goes from ground to air. The hen lays reddish eggs in a pit in the ground and assumes sole responsibility for brooding, while the cock stands guard and fetch food. The cock is extremely brave in fighting off any intruders. As resident birds, the capercaillies build their homes in the Greater Hinggan Mountains, but in recent years they have been moving their habitat northward, deeper into the forests, in the face of encroaching lumbering squads.

Severtzov's hazel grouse (*Bonasia sewerzowi*) is found only in the Chinese provinces of Gansu, Qinghai and Sichuan. It likes to live in dragon spruce, red alder or clethra forests and shrubs where it can find both food and cover. The bird is no bigger than a crow, with grey, spotted plumage and a crest. It is timid and vigilant, ready to take flight before the enemy approaches. Small groups of hazel grouse feed on tender grass and berries in summer and in winter feed on tender tree leaves and buds. Because of its habit of living in trees in winter, its toes grow a covering of hornlike pimples, as if it were wearing a pair of sports shoes to prevent it from slipping on the branches. Late in April it builds its nest in shrubs and lays eggs. The nest is very crude but ingeniously camouflaged.

The willow ptarmigan is found only in Heilongjiang and Xinjiang in China. It is accustomed to tundra surroundings. Its plumage is grey during breeding and white in winter as a protective colour in snow. It is a typical frigid-zone bird, living in young birch forests, tundra intermingled with pine groves, mixed birch forests, groves of broad-leaved trees, willow groves or red alder forests in summer and autumn. The willow ptarmigans in China do not migrate. They gather in groups after autumn and live under the snow in winter. They have a feather covering on their tarsi, presumably as protection from cold. This, plus the lack of spurs on their feet, distinguishes them from other birds.

The following chart shows the distribution of the forty-nine pheasant species in China:

Geographical Distribution of Pheasant Species in China

	Species	NE*	NC	MX	QT	SW	CC	SC
Partridges	Alectoris graeca		+	+				
	Arborophila ardens							+
	Arborophila atrogularis					+		
	Arborophila chloropus							+
	Arborophila crudigularis							+
	Arborophila gingica							+
	Arborophila javanica							+
	Arborophila mandellii					+		
	Arborophila rufipectus					+		
	Arborophila rufogularis					+		+
	Arborophila torqueola					+		
	Bambusicola fytchii					+		
	Bambusicola thoracica					+	+	+
	Coturnix chinensis							+
	Coturnix coturnix	+		+				
	Francolinus pintadeanus							+
	Ithaginis cruentus					+		

	Species	NE	NC	MX	QT	SW	CC	SC
Patridges	*Lerwa Lerwa*				+	+		
	Perdix dauuricae	+	+	+				
	Perdix hodgsoniae			+	+	+		
	Perdix perdix	+						
	Tetraogallus himalayensis			+	+			
	Tetraogallus tibetanus				+			
	Tetraophasis obscurus				+	+		
	Tragopan blythii					+		
	Tragopan caboti						+	
	Tragopan melanocephalus				+			
	Tragopan satyra				+			
	Tragopan temminckii					+	+	

	Species	NE	CN	MX	QT	SW	CC	SC
Pheasants	*Chrysolophus amherstiae*					+		
	Chrysolophus pictus					+	+	
	Crossoptilon auritum			+		+		
	Crossoptilon crossoptilon				+	+		
	Crossoptilon mantchuricum		+					
	Gallus gallus							+
	Lophophorus impejanus				+			
	Lophophorus lhuysii					+		
	Lophophorus sclateri					+		
	Lophura leucomelana					+		
	Lophura nycthemera					+	+	+
	Lophura swinhoei							+
	Pavo muticus					+		
	Phasianus colchicus	+	+	+	+	+	+	+
	Polyplectron bicalcaratum							+
	Pucrasia macrolopha		+			+	+	
	Syrmaticus ellioti						+	
	Syrmaticus humiae					+		
	Syrmaticus mikado							+
	Syrmaticus reevesii		+			+		

* NE=northeast China; NC=north China; MX=Inner Mongolia and Xinjiang region; QT=Qinghai and Tibet region; SW=southwest China; CC=central China; SC=south China.

Quite a number of the species are endemic to certain geographical zones of China, such as the brown eared pheasant (*Crossoptilon mantchuricum*) of north China; the blue eared pheasant (*C. auritum*) of Inner Mongolia; the pheasant grouse (*Tetraophasis obscurus*) and the white eared pheasant (*Crossoptilon crossoptilon*) of Tibet and Qinghai; the blood pheasant (*Ithaginis cruentus*), the Chinese monal (*Lophophorus lhuysii*) and the silver pheasant (*Lophura nycthemera*) of southwest China; the Fukien tragopan (*Tragopan caboti*) and the golden pheasant (*Chrysolophus pictus*) of central China; the Hainan hill partridge (*Arborophila ardens*) and the Taiwan blue pheasant (*Lophura swinhoei*) of south China. Southwest China leads other parts of China in the number of pheasant species — twenty-four — hence its name "the paradize of pheasants." Northeast China has only four species of pheasants but has an advantage in numbers, so the region is known as the pheasant game region. There are also some small, short-winged species of pheasants, notably the common quail (*Coturnix coturnix*), the Chinese francolin (*Francolinus pintadeanus*), the Chukor partridge (*Alectoris graeca*), the valuable blood pheasant (*Ithaginis cruentus*), and the tragopans (*Tragopan*).

The common quail reproduces in northeast China and Xinjiang and migrates all over China. It is the size of a chick, with long, pointed wings and a short tail. The feathers on its back are mostly dark brown with light yellow stripes. It is reddish brown on the lower neck and greyish white on the abdomen. The Ming Dynasty physician Li Shizhen (1518 - 1593) describes the bird in his *Outline of Herb Medicine* as "residing on field ridges, flying in groups at night and hidden in grass during the day." This shows the common quail frequents grass and fields in search of food, preferring dry land near water but sometimes found in thin woods, vast grasslands or fields. It migrates in flocks in autumn, usually on moonlit nights. If chased, quail often scatter over short distances, then hide in grass. If chased again, they hastily take flight.

After reaching their breeding ground in spring, they begin crowing. The cock is bellicose, but its crow is rather weak. Quail usually build their nests of dry leaves and grass on dry patches of grassland; a brood generally consists of nine to eleven eggs. The eggs very greatly in colour, ranging from yellowish white to light brown and covered with brown spots of varying sizes. Raised domestically, the common quail lays eggs almost every day. If allowed to lay eggs continuously, the hen cannot live long — one or two years. The quail egg is similar to the chicken egg, containing protein, fat, hydrocarbonates, phosphorus, calcium, iron, etc., but in China it is believed that quail eggs are particularly nutritious. In the old days people made use of the bellicosity of the quail and trained them for quail fights.

The Chinese francolin is resident in the southern provinces of China. It looks like a chicken but is smaller. Its dark crest is encircled with a reddish-brown ring; both upperparts and underparts are dark with round white spots. It usually moves among bushes on low hills. Its wings are round and short, limiting it to short distances in flight, but it flies very fast. It is very vigilant and whenever frightened, hides deep in a bush. Its crow is heard the year round, a clear and loud "*hee — hee — hee — ga — ga.*" It lowers its head for the "*hee — hee*" and raises it for the "*ga — ga.*" When the wooded hills are in full spring bloom on Hainan Island, Chinese francolins are crowing everywhere for mating. A cock tends to occupy a hill, not letting others encroach upon its territory. The Chinese francolin is omnivorous, feeding on insects as well as berries, grass seed and tender leaves. In Guangdong and Hainan the bird lays eggs twice a year, with each brood consisting of three to six eggs. The eggs are white or creamy yellow and look like a pear.

Because the Chinese francolin crows with a wailing drawl, some Chinese scholars in the past chose to believe it was a sad bird. "Hills shrouded in gloomy autumn moon, from branches of bitter bamboo francolins fly," the Tang Dynasty poet Li Bai (701 - 762) wrote. "Hill partridge, why are you crowing so bitterly till dawn, since you never leave your village, your flock or your nest?" queried another poet, Bai Juyi (772 - 846). [The Chinese francolin and the hill partridge bear the same name, *zhegu*, in Chinese.] The hill partridge is also raised as a game bird, and southerners treasure it for its meat. People in Fujian say, "A delicacy from the mountains is the partridge and from the sea, the mackerel." Nowadays ornithologists are demanding that a game law be enacted to ban hunting of valuable birds in certain seasons so as to protect the propagation of the francolin and hill partridge. The Hainan hill partridge (*Arborophila ardens*), the Taiwan hill partridge (*A. crudigularis*) and the Sichuan hill partridge (*A. rufipectus*), all peculiar to China and found in very limited regions, should be preserved with great care.

The blood pheasant is found in high mountains near the snow line in Tibet, Sichuan and a vast area from the northwestern part of Yunnan Province in the south to the Qilian Mountains in Qinghai and Gansu and the Qinling Mountains in Shaanxi in the north. It moves to an altitude between 3,300 and 4,500 metres in summer and to around 2,900 metres in winter. Such a drastic vertical migration obviously has something to do with the movement of the snow line.

The blood pheasant usually moves about

in conifers or bushes in a flock of four or five to twenty. The woods are usually quiet, cool places. Poor at flying, the blood pheasant just runs away from its enemy. Its food consists mainly of green plants and seeds, such as the leaves or seeds of moss, cypress and arrow bamboo. The breeding season is between late April and June, during which the birds separate into pairs. The hen selects a covered depression in bushes, under rocks or beside a fallen tree. She carries fallen leaves, fine roots or moss to the place, presses them down with her body and proceeds to lay eggs. The hatching period usually lasts for twenty-nine days, after which the parents live with their young until winter. The blood pheasant's habitat is cold, high mountains; in plains it usually survives for about one year.

There are five species of tragopans in China. They are rare birds and all five species are under protection.

Tragopans are distributed widely in China, from the Himalayas in Tibet to coastal Fujian Province. The male has a crest on its head and two horns above the eyes, which earn the bird its name of horned pheasant. In the breeding season the throat of the male is covered with a loose lappet that hangs down brightly in time of passion. The face and throat are naked or sparsely covered with fine feathers. The female is mostly varying shades of brown.

The Fukien tragopan (*Tragopan caboti*) is called the yellow-bellied horned pheasant in Chinese because of a yellow patch on its abdomen. The Fukien tragopan is a Chinese specialty whose distribution is limited to central and northwest Fujian, northern Guangdong and southeast Hunan. The male is chestnut with round yellow dots and its underparts are buff. Living in high mountains at an altitude between 1,000 and 1,600 metres above sea level, the Fukien tragopan is difficult to raise and breed.

The Chinese tragopan (*Tragopan temminckii*) is called the red bellied horned pheasant in Chinese for its red underparts. It is also called the grey-spotted horned pheasant. It is found in fir and red birch forests in the northern part of Sichuan and Yunnan and in the mountains of Shaanxi, Hubei and Hunan. The bird lives under cover of thick bushes of rhododendron and arrow bamboo or on moss-covered tree trunks. It usually moves singly. In time of passion the lappet under its throat grows and shows a pattern resembling the Chinese character *shou*, meaning longevity, hence yet another name, the longevity pheasant. The beautiful male bird is prized as a pet. It was taken to Europe as a rare bird a century ago.

Pheasants, which make up the greater part of the Phasianidae family, are bigger and have longer tail feathers than partridges. The family includes such valuable species as the monal, the eared pheasant, the silver pheasant, the golden pheasant, the copper pheasant and peafowl as well as game birds, such as the China pheasant and Chukor partridge.

The male monal is characterized by the metallic tint of its plumage. China is the main habitat for the monal — from the Himalayas in Tibet through northwest Yunnan, western Sichuan, southern Gansu and southeast Qinghai.

The Chinese monal (*Lophophorus lhuysii*) has a bluish-green tail. It usually moves about in small groups in woods or on tundra of rocky highlands at altitudes between 4,000 and 5,000 metres above sea level and moves lower in winter. At night it shelters in pines or thick rhododendron bushes. It digs into the earth with its beak to eat tender roots or tubers, especially the tuber of fritillary. Under artificial rearing it usually lays a brood of three to five eggs, which are dark brown covered with purplish spots. The bird contracts diseases easily and therefore is difficult to raise.

There are three species of eared pheasants — the brown eared pheasant (*Crossoptilon mantchuricum*), the white eared pheasant (*C. crossoptilon*) and the blue eared pheasant (*C. auritum*), all resident in China. The eared pheasant has a pair of long, slightly stiff ear coverts and its central rectrices hang down loosely like a horsetail. The male and female are exactly the same except for short, thick spurs on the feet of the male.

Brown eared pheasants are very limited in population number and their distribution is confined to the mountainous regions of northwest Shanxi and Hebei. The bird in the wild is on the verge of extinction in Hebei Province as a result of wanton felling of trees. The brown eared pheasant is dark brown all over with white auriculars and loosely hanging tail feathers. It resides in wooded rolling hills, usually in groups of thirty or so. When frightened, the bird scurries to the ridge of a hill before taking wing and gliding down the valley or the slope on the other side of the hill. When it crows, it stretches its neck and raises its tail with the two central rectrices very erect. In mating, only one cock pairs with one hen, so fights are frequent among the males during mating time in spring. Because the male brown eared pheasant literally fights to the death, Chinese emperors in the past chose the tail feathers of the bird to adorn the helmets of their generals as a symbol of bravery.

The brown eared pheasant feeds on tubers and tender roots and occasionally on insects.

The blue eared pheasant is a rare bird resident in northwest China, inhabiting the Qilian Mountains in Qinghai and Gansu provinces and the Helan Mountains in Ningxia. The bird earns its name from its greyish-blue body.

Top: capercaillie; *centre right*: hazel grouse; *centre left*: willow ptarmigan in summer plumage; *bottom*: willow ptarmigan in winter plumage.

Top: brown eared pheasant; *centre*: white eared pheasant; *bottom*: blue eared pheasant.

Reevesii pheasant (*upper right*); Mikado pheasant (*left*); blood pheasant.

Green peafowl.

Golden pheasant.

Tragopan.

Monal pheasant.

Chinese copper pheasant.

Silver pheasant.

The white eared pheasant is also limited to China, mainly in western Sichuan, southern Qinghai and eastern Tibet. The body is virtually white with particularly long, erect tail feathers.

The silver pheasant (*Lophura nycthemera*) is a beautiful bird too. Li Bai, the Tang Dynasty poet, was a great lover of birds. Once when he was on a tour of scenic Huangshan (Yellow Mountain), he learned that a family named Hu had raised a pair of silver pheasants. The poet immediately called on the elder Hu and admired the birds immensely. The old peasant happened to be an admirer of Li Bai's, so he gave the pheasants to the poet and asked for a poem in return. The overjoyed poet composed a poem on the spot. This episode shows that the Chinese people reared silver pheasants as early as the Tang Dynasty (618 – 907). Silver pheasants are distributed mainly in southern China, but also in Burma, Thailand and the Indochinese peninsula. There are thirteen subspecies of the silver pheasant, eight of which reside in China.

The silver pheasant has white upperparts with fine, dark stripes and dark-blue underparts. It lives in southern mountainous provinces, especially in thick bamboo groves up to an altitude of 1,500 metres above sea level. It moves about on the ground during the day, nestles in trees at night and wanders about in search of food in the morning. It has a habit of scratching the ground with its toes and washes its feathers with sand. It runs off if frightened, but when it reaches a safe distance, it keeps looking back as it walks along. When running, it holds its crest erect and raises its tail feathers. During the mating season one male mates with several females. The cock is very bellicose. The hen builds its nest in depressions in bushy areas and lays four to six eggs. The silver pheasant is mentioned in ancient Chinese poetry and other literary works.

The Taiwan blue pheasant (*Lophura swinhoei*), limited to mountains in Taiwan, is also a Chinese specialty. Similar to the silver pheasant in shape, the blue pheasant is mostly dark blue. The Kalij pheasant (*Lophura leucomelana*) is about the size of the silver pheasant, but the male is almost entirely black and the female is mainly reddish brown. The Kalij pheasant is also rare, found only in the Himalayas in China.

The red junglefowl (*Gallus gallus*) is the predecessor of the domestic chicken. Bones of the red junglefowl have been found in the Miaodigou ruins, dating from 2500 B.C., at Sanmenxia, Henan Province. Pottery chickens patterned after domestic chickens have been discovered at the Qujialing ruins in the Yangtze valley. These findings show that domestication of the junglefowl in China has a history of at least 3,000 years.

The red junglefowl is still found in subtropical jungles in the southern parts of Yunnan and Guangxi and on Hainan Island in Guangdong Province. The birds, in threes or fours, search for food in the woods after sunrise. Like its domestic cousin, the red junglefowl scratches the ground with its feet and pecks at insects while walking. It hides in bushes in shady woods at noon when the sun beats down fiercely. Sometimes it digs a nest in the ground or rolls in sand to take a "sandbath." It becomes lively again when dusk falls, walking around, seeking food. It takes shelter in groups in nearby trees at night. The male crows like the domestic cock with a "*gu - gu - gu — gu.*"

Domestication of the junglefowl in China is marked not only by its long history but also by the large number of fine varieties. A "yellow" chicken, first bred in Hebei and Shandong provinces, is a good table bird as the cock may grow to a body weight of 6 kilograms and a hen to 4.5 kg.

The yellow chicken is prized for its tender meat. There are also a number of good egg-and-meat varieties, such as the Shouguang, Langshan, Fudong, Big-Bone and Beijing Fat. The Taihe Black is important in traditional Chinese medicine. It has white feathers and black skin, bones and flesh. The meat, though dark, is delicious. It is indispensable in a Chinese medicinal preparation called Pill of Black Chick — White Phoenix — a tonic for women.

Long-tailed pheasants (Syrmaticus) are also found only in China and have been recorded in northern and western Hebei, southern Shanxi and Shaanxi, northern Hubei, Hunan and Guizhou, western Henan and Anhui, and eastern Sichuan. They are about the size of the common pheasant, but the tail feathers are much longer and are used for the headwear of ancient generals in Peking opera.

Long-tailed pheasants live in steep valleys of 600-metre-high mountains, feeding on seeds of pines and other conifers. They can fly long distances and can stop abruptly in the middle of fast flight by using their long tails to turn their bodies around and resist the air currents with their spread wings and tail, then turning the head downward and landing in a tree. When frightened, they utter loud cries. Under domestication they often crow at a high pitch, sometimes with a beautiful trill.

The golden pheasant (Chrysolophus puctus) is another bird found only in China — in southeast Qinghai, southern Gansu and Shaanxi, western Sichuan, Guizhou and Hunan, and eastern Guangxi. It is found in greatest numbers in the Qinling Mountains near Baoji City in Shaanxi Province, hence the city's name, Baoji, meaning "treasured chicken."

The golden pheasant lives on hilly terraces or steep cliffs, appears in bushes and bamboo groves during the day and sleeps on the lower branches of trees no higher than four metres from the ground. In winter, especially after a snowfall, when food is scarce in the mountains, it leaves the mountains in groups to seek food in the terraced fields where the snow has melted. In the evening it returns to the mountains to pass the night in its old habitat, perching on high branches. When it goes up or down hill, it hops along its familiar path until it reaches a rocky gully or clearing, when it half spreads its wings and glides. Its food consists mainly of ferns, grass seed, peas, wild dates and garlic. In heat the cock dances gracefully in curves or circles around the hen. Occasionally it turns around and starts dancing in the opposite direction. While flirting with the hen, the cock moves in little trots and gives out low cries. Such courting rituals may last for three to five seconds or as long as twenty-five seconds, depending on how much the hen moves about.

The Chinese copper pheasant (Chrysolophus amherstiae) is also called the white-bellied pheasant. People in Sichuan call it the bamboo-shoot pheasant because it eats a lot of bamboo shoots. It is also called the qin pheasant by people in Yunnan Province because of its gorgeous plumage, for qin in Chinese means quilt. The bird is distributed in south-central Sichuan and the greater part of Yunnan. Its brilliant plumage is comparable to that of the golden pheasant. The male has a metallic saphire head, back and breast, with a purple crest and white shoulders. Each feather has a black edge. The bird's underparts are vermilion, and the tail is a cloud pattern of black and white. The belly is white. The female has brown upperparts and tail and a nearly pure white belly.

The Chinese copper pheasant lives in mountains at altitudes ranging from 2,000 to 4,000 metres above sea level, much higher and farther south than the habitat of the golden pheasant. It is found mostly in thorn bushes and dwarf bamboo groves on poor hills instead of in thick woods. It moves about singly or in pairs, but in winter in groups of twenty to thirty. In domestication it mates easily with the golden pheasant and produces a great variety of hybrids.

The bird was introduced into Europe as early as 1828 and was much sought after for its gorgeous plumage, bringing as much as U.S. $ 800 up to 1873. Today the bird is raised in and outside China. It usually lives for twenty months, but some live as long as eight years.

The peafowl falls into two categories — the green and the blue. The green peafowl (*Pavo muticus*) is found in southern Yunnan in China and also in Bangladesh, Burma and Thailand. The blue peafowl (*Pavo cristatus*) lives in India and Sri Lanka. In China the green peafowl is under state protection and is a symbol of beauty in literature and the arts.

The peafowl is a big-bodied species in the Phasianidae family. A cluster of crest feathers stands upright. The bird is not capable of flying because of its short wings. However, it has strong, stocky legs capable of walking. With sharp claws, the peafowl is good at finding food by scratching the ground the way the domestic chicken does. It has a medium-length beak with the downward-curving upper, bill longer than the lower one. The head of the peacock is covered with fine, dark-green feathers to form the crown. The face is light yellow; the dark-green head and upper neck shine with a purplish tint. The feathers on the back are the colour of green jade; each feather has a dark edge and an oval bronze pattern in the centre. The breast feathers are greenish, and those on the belly, dark brown. The not very large wings are covered with yellowish-brown, dark-blue and fresh-green feathers. The most gorgeous part of the peacock is its upper tail coverts, which can be twice as long as its body length. The tail feathers are actually not very long. The upper tail coverts have fine, golden-green barbs with copper-colour tips. Some of the upper tail coverts have golden-green ocelli. The rest of the coverts end in yellow forks. When a peacock dances around a peahen, all its upper tail coverts spread upward with the forked coverts and eye-patterned ones arranged in a dazzling folding fan. The eye-patterned coverts are brilliant, reflecting the light like a myriad mirrors. The Chinese say, "The peacock is displaying its beauty."

People often find bundles of peafowl feathers in the forests of southern Yunnan Province. These are left by the bird after it changes its plumage. In ancient times in China people used peacock feathers to make fans or weave into clothes or even into the cover of the imperial sedan.

The commonest of all the economic species of pheasants in China is the common, or ring-necked, pheasant (*Phasianus colchicus*), which is also called the mountain pheasant in China. Its distribution is far and wide — almost all over the country except for Hainan Island in Guangdong and the Qiangtang district of Tibet. The bird lives in fixed areas and never migrates. It likes to stay in grass on hills or high mountains in summer and moves to nearby flat grassland in winter. The male and female differ vastly in appearance. While the cock has gorgeous plumage of metallic yellow, red-copper, white and bluish green, with a white ring around its neck, the hen is mostly a nonmetallic yellowish brown with some chestnut dots. The cock has a pair of long tail feathers — half again as long as the body — with colourful patterns. The tail of the hen is much shorter. The cock is also armed with a very strong hornlike spur on the back of each foot, which it uses as its weapon in fighting. The breeding season begins in March, with a one-month difference between northern and southern parts of the country. The hen builds its nest on the ground in surroundings of colour similar to its plumage.

The common pheasant is a major game bird in China. Its meat is more delicious than that of the domestic chicken. There is a good supply on the market around Spring Festival. Its plumes, especially the tail feathers, are sought after as ornaments and material for handicrafts. In the interests of preservation, overhunting should be prohibited, particularly of the hens during the breeding season.

The Chukor partridge (*Alectoris graeca*) is a bit bigger than the quail. It has short tail feathers and is brownish grey bordering on reddish brown on the head and upperparts and yellowish brown on the underparts. A dark ring runs from its forehead through the eyes down to the breast, looking like a lady's necklace. Its cry sounds like "*ga—ga*," so it is also called the *gaga* pheasant in some parts of China. The bird is fat, its meat is tender and it grows in large numbers in a vast region in China. People think the bird is stupid, because it hides under a rock, thinking it is free from danger. When it is hidden in such a place and sings to its heart's content, it invariably finds it's too late to flee when an enemy makes a surprise attack. People also use captured Chukor partridges as decoys to lure more of them.

Section V

Raptores (Birds of Prey)

All birds of prey have sharp hooked beaks and talons and strong wings, enabling them to prey on other animals. Birds of prey fall into two categories, the diurnal, such as the eagle, falcon and vulture, and the nocturnal, such the owl and barn owl. Quite a number of valuable species of diurnal birds of prey live in China. Their feathers are of high economic value, particularly the wing and tail feathers. Although a few prey on wild ducks and domestic fowl, most of them feed mainly on rodents, so they are also useful to farming. The hunting of eagles and falcons should be strictly controlled.

The red-legged falcon (*Falco vespertinus*) is about the size of a pigeon. The male has a grey back and red legs and feet. The bird flies very fast and is also called the grey swallow in China. When the bird comes to China to breed during spring and summer, it likes to occupy magpie nests. The two birds often fight over the nest for days. Sometimes red-legged falcons make nests for themselves, mostly in trees, never on rocks. In the summer they fly over the plain, very often seeming to poise in midair, head down. When they see food on the ground, they shoot down. They fly over the fields in search of food till dusk. The bird is loved by farmers because it feeds mainly on locusts and mole crickets.

The peregrine falcon (*Falco peregrinus*) has another name in China—the duck's tiger—an indication that ducks are its main prey. It usually attacks a wild duck in flight by striking it with its feet. If the first attempt misses the target, the falcon rises to a higher altitude and mounts another attack until it gets its prey. When diving, it can reach a speed of 75 to 100 metres per second. The dive is usually at a 25-degree angle. After it has brought its prey down to the ground, the peregrine falcon slits the duck's throat with its sharp beaks, then pierces its backbone. Sometimes it takes its prey to a shelter, then kills it. If the captive has only fainted and not died, it will struggle to get free when it comes to. At this, the

Little owl.

Golden eagle (*top*), red-footed falcon (*centre right*), Steeler's sea eagle (*centre left*), bearded vulture.

peregrine falcon waits for its prey to quiet down, then pecks at its throat several times with its sharp beak until the captive dies from loss of blood. As a rule, the peregrine falcon strips feathers and skin from the wild duck, then tears its flesh to pieces before eating it. The peregrine falcon also preys on greenfinches and dusky thrushes. It builds its nest in cliff crevices, but sometimes it also lays eggs on the ground.

The golden eagle (*Aquila chrysaetos*) is the biggest, quite frequently seen eagle in China. It is covered almost entirely with chestnut feathers, except for white splashes under the wings that become conspicuous during flight. Its habitat is mainly mountains and grasslands and rarely plains. It flies fast, often gliding in a straight line or in a spiral. The white feathers from its wings and tail are used for making fans.

Pallas's fish eagle (*Haliaeetus leucoryphus*) is also one of the bigger eagles. It is dark brown except for a wide white stripe on its tail that gives it its name of jade-belt eagle in China. The tail feathers are valuable ornaments. The bird is found in northwest China and southeastern coastal regions.

The white-tailed sea eagle (*Haliaeetus albicilla*) visits coastal regions during its breeding season, but otherwise lives in high mountains or on grasslands far away from the sea. The bird mostly lives alone but is seen with its young after the breeding season. It flies fairly slowly, with great ease, alighting on a rock, the ground or a tree branch to rest. Its wing and tail feathers are of commercial value.

The Kamchatkan sea eagle (*Haliaeerus pelagicus*), large, brown with a thick beak, is a relatively rare bird, visiting a few spots on the northern coast of China. During flight it glides in circles. It is also sometimes een resting on coastal sand dunes or on oig trees on a lakeshore. Its feathers are prized. Eagles usually have twelve tail feathers each, but the Kamchatkan sea feathers each, but the Kamchatkan sea eagle has fourteen, which fetch a good price.

The osprey (*Pandion haliaeetus*) is also called fish eagle in China, because it preys on fish. Its outer toes can turn backward and there are scales under the toes and beside the claws that facilitate its catching fish. It is seen frequently in rivers, lakes and on coasts. Sometimes it flies high in the air and sometimes it flies low over the water in search of fish.

The black kite (*Milvus korschun*) is dark brown all over with a white spot under each wing. When the bird is flying, its tail spreads in a fork, unlike other birds of prey, which all have round tails when in flight. The black kite is found all over China. On a fine day people in town and countryside see the black kite above. In winter black kites fly long distances in threes and fours. One flap of the wings carries the bird forward for such a distance that it seems to hang in midair. It has sharp eyes. The moment it spots something edible on the ground, it plummets down with a piercing cry that turns into a trembling drawl, as if blowing a pipe.

The vulture is known for eating animal carcasses. The species seen in Tibet and Xinjiang in China is the bearded vulture (*Gypaetus barbatus*). It has a big beak, crooked talons and a cluster of fine, black feathers under its chin that looks like a beard, hence its name. The upperparts are black, whereas the quills are white. The throat, breast, belly, the rest of the underparts and the under-tail coverts are creamy, except for those of old vultures which are rusty. The change in colour is attributed to the bird's stay on high cliffs that are mostly rich in ferric oxide quartz. The corrosive ferric oxide soils the feathers, particularly when the air is damp. Because the vulture flies high and often rests on mountain peaks, some peaks in China are named vulture peak.

The commonest nocturnal bird of prey

is the owl. The Scops owl (*Otus scops*) is common in China. Because it is active at night and its head looks like that of a cat, it is also called night cat in China.

The Scops owl is greyish brown throughout with some dark-brown spots. The ear tufts are obvious, and fine feathers radiate from the big eges to form a face frame, helpful at night in determining the direction of sound. The visual cells of the owl are almost entirely cylindroid cells, which are sensitive to light only at night, and its auriculars also enable it to collect sound waves at night.

The Chinese of old considered the owl an inauspicious animal, partly because of its frightening appearance and partly because of its loud, miserable cry. But the owl is a very useful bird. It is estimated that an owl is capable of capturing two or three rats every night, or about a thousand rats a year, and that means about five tons of grain saved.

Section VI

Columbidae and Scansores (Pigeons, Parrots, Cuckoos and Others)

Most of these are resident birds. They have short bills with a soft base. They mainly live in trees and are good at flying. Their gular pouches produce milk for their fledgelings. The commonest among them are the blue hill pigeon and the turtledove.

Pallas's sand grouse (*Syrrhaptes paradoxus*) belongs to the pigeon family, although it is called a grouse. Sand grouses winter in the Inner Mongolian Autonomous Region of China. A perplexing phenomenon is that the birds often kill themselves

by dashing against tree trunks or electricity poles. Pallas's sand grouse is a typical desert bird with legs covered with a thick layer of long, fine down, so it is also called the hairy-legged sand grouse in China. The bird is a little bigger than the quail. As a winter migrant, it passes the summer in Europe and visits Inner Mongolia in winter. After arriving in the desert, the flock does not disband but goes on living and feeding in groups.

The bird has a small head and thin, short legs with three toes joining at the base. Under its heels there are thick, rough skin and a small growth. It cannot run fast or fly high; it can only fly low in a straight line over a short distance. Both its sight and hearing are very poor. When flying in a flock, the lead bird is so inept that it often fails to detour around an obstacle; instead it leads the others into it, causing their deaths.

The blue hill pigeon (*Columba rupestris*) is also called the wild pigeon in China. It is different from the domestic pigeon. The bird has two transverse white stripes, one at the rump and the other near the tip of the tail.

Domestication of the pigeon has a long history in China; there are over one hundred varieties. The high-rump pigeon has a rump as round as a ball, and the somersaulting pigeon likes to somersault in the air. Some mass organizations sponsor pigeon flight contests. The longest distance was 1,715 kilometres between Shanghai and Lanzhou. Carrier pigeons are trained not only by the army but also by individuals in China.

The thick-billed pigeon (*Treron curvirostra*) is covered with green plumage. It likes the thick, moist jungles of subtropical and tropical Hainan Island and Yunnan Province. It relishes the fruit of banyan trees, so where there are banyan forests, there are thick-billed pigeons. The female

Top to bottom: blue hill pigeon, green pigeon, cuckoo, hoopoe.

Top to bottom: swift, red-rumped swallow, barn swallow.

Great pied hornbill (*above*), kingfisher.

Parakeet.

Woodpecker.

and male work together to build their nest on crisscrossing or vine-entangled branches about two to three metres above ground or even lower. The nest, made of straw or twigs, is so crude that eggs can be seen from below. The birds are bellicose during brooding, so it is very rare to find two nests adjoining each other. Intruders are rebuffed, but man may approach a nest when the female is brooding. Even if frightened away, it will return a moment later.

Climbing birds are endowed with two forward toes and two backward toes on each foot that facilitate resting perpendicularly on a tree. They include kingfishers, which feed on fish; cuckoos, which feed on caterpillars; woodpeckers, which pick insects from tree bark; and parrots, which mimic human language.

Parrots are distributed in South Asia, Oceania, Africa, and Central and South America. In China the common species is the red-breasted parakeet (*Psittacula alexandri*), which has gorgeous plumage of green upperparts and red underparts. It feeds on berries, nuts and other fruit as well as tender buds. Parrots often move about in large groups of up to several hundred. They pass the night in trees with mynas, crows and other birds. Endowed with a thick, soft tongue, the parrot is capable of imitating the human voice.

The hoopoe (*Upupa epops*) is a beautiful bird with a feather crest and brown plumage with transverse white stripes. When it cries, its crest spreads into a brilliant fan, so it is also called the cockscomb bird. Its cry sounds like "hoo-po-po," so yet another name is hoopopo. Beautiful though it is, the bird is lazy and cares little about cleanliness. It often lays its eggs in the hole of the woodpecker. Sometimes it lays its eggs just in litter or on structures near houses. Its nest is dirty and foul. No other bird would return to a tree hole or a nest once occupied by the hoopoe because

of the stench. The young of the hoopoe emits a smelly green liquid. The hoopoe frequents orchards and vegetable gardens and kills wireworms, mole crickets and other pests.

The cuckoo (*Cuculus*) is also called the *buku* in Chinese. Like *cuckoo* in English, *coucou* in French and *Kuckuk* in German, the name is derived from its call. The bird's rhythmic call is heard on the east China coast late in spring and early in summer. The cuckoo is timid and hides deep in the forest. Its feathers are dull, with black stripes on the belly and a dark-brown tail that is white at the tip. The cuckoo calls repeatedly at night, even all night when there is moonlight. Chinese poets in ancient times often wrote about the call of the bird to convey sadness at the departure of spring. The Chinese name for cuckoo is the same as that for rhododendron, because an ancient Chinese poet imagined that while the cuckoo was calling all night, it must surely have been bleeding, and its blood stained the rhododendron red.

Building nests and nursing the young are common instincts for most birds, but the cuckoo is an exception. When the female is going to lay an egg, it just waits beside the nest of other birds. When the female in that nest leaves, the cuckoo promptly gets into the nest, takes out an egg, lays an egg of its own, then flies away. When the cuckoo egg is hatched by the other bird, the young cuckoo is fed by its stepparents. The young cuckoo has sensitive cells on its back. When it comes into contact with the other fledgelings or eggs in the nest, it often repulses them, Squeezing them out of the nest so they drop dead on the ground. The cuckoo is often hatched before the others. After being fed by its fosterparents for some time, it grows big enough to leave the nest. Its real parents, who have stayed in the vicinity, instantly take it away.

The cuckoo is a great eater of worms and therefore does much good for farming. A cuckoo fledgeling may eat thirty-nine locusts or fifty pine caterpillars a day, and an adult can eat a hundred pine caterpillars an hour. Many birds dare not touch hairy worms, but the cuckoo is very good at pecking at such worms. The bird indeed deserves protection.

All four toes on each foot of the large white-rumped swift (*Apus pacificus*) point forward, so it can rest perpendicularly only on cliffs or tree trunks. It cannot rest on branches or electric wires or walk on the ground, but its large, long wings make it one of the fastest birds, capable of flying 150 to 160 kilometres an hour. When winter is over, the white-rumped swift is among the first birds to announce the arrival of spring to the Chinese people. It passes the winter in Australia and Southeast Asia and returns to China in the spring. It builds its nest on city walls, old pagodas or under the eaves of temples as well as in the crevices of cliffs. Its saucer-like nest is made of mud, straw and rags padded with down. When swifts are not mating, laying eggs or brooding, they spend almost the whole day in the sky catching worms. When a swift catches a worm, it keeps it in its mouth until it collects enough worms to make into a ball before swallowing it. Because the swift can only hang from a cliff or a tree trunk, it is very difficult for it to take off. To do so, it has to drop into the air and fall two to three metres before it can spread its wings and take flight. While other birds hasten to take shelter from rain, the swifts gleefully chase each other in a light rain, calling "gee-gee."

Kingfishers (*Halcyon*) were first mentioned in China in *Huainanzi*, annotated by Gao You, a book of the Han Dynasty (206 B.C.--A.D. 220) on philosophy and natural history. The Tang Dynasty poet Li Shangyin (circa 813-858) mentioned the bird in one of his poems, calling it *feicui*, which today is also the name of a brilliant green jade stone. The kingfisher has brilliant green plumage with a brown belly. It often stands still beside a river for a long time. The moment it spots fish or shrimp swimming by, it springs into action, plunging into the water to snag its food by its bill. Sometimes it hovers some five to seven metres above the water. When it has caught a fish or shrimp, it flies away swiftly in a straight line with high-pitched cries. It builds its nest by digging a 60-centimetre tunnel in the sandy bank of a field. It lays six or seven white, smooth eggs. Because of its brilliance, the plumage of the kingfisher was used by the Chinese imperial family to make the queen's phoenix crown or was woven into the emperor's robe.

The great pied hornbill (*Buceros bicornis*) is a rare bird in China, found in the southern part of Yunnan Province. With its conspicuous hornbill, it flies clumsily. Hornbills often fly in flocks, one behind the other, flapping their wings several times, then gliding forward. Because the underwing coverts do not cover the base of the remiges, the remiges make quite a big noise when in flight. A peculiarity of the hornbill is that the female is sealed in a tree hole while hatching and nursing the young. The male collects shells of nuts and seeds and both birds seal the entrance to the tree hole with these materials and a sticky liquid emitted from their stomachs. Only a small crevice is left unsealed to allow the female to thrust her head out to be fed by the male. When the male can no longer feed both mother and fledgelings, the mother breaks the entrance with her bill and leaves the hole. Then the entrance is reduced to a small crevice again and both male and female feed the young through the crevice. This sealing of the entrance to the tree hole is obviously meant to guard against hostile intruders, such as monkeys and snakes.

The Indian jungle nightjar (*Caprimulgus*

indicus) is greyish brown over most of its body with vermiculation transverse stripes. It comes out mostly at night and is particularly active at sundown. It flaps its wings slowly and quietly and sometimes just glides forward, continuously catching insects in flight. During daytime the bird squats on a branch or on the ground of thick forests. As its feathers match the colour of tree bark, it is very difficult to discern it when it is in a tree. Sometimes at night the bird squats on the road with its beak wide open and its eyes shining in the dark. In the past people thought the bird hid among goats in order to steal the goats' milk, hence its other name in Europe, the Goatsucker. This is obviously a misunderstanding. However, its big beak is indeed convenient for catching large winged moths. The bird is very common in the eastern part of China. Recent observation shows that the Indian jungle nightjar "hibernates" to tide over the food-scarce winter.

The woodpecker (*Picus*) is called the forest doctor, not only because it kills worms underneath the tree bark, but also because its holes indicate which trees are healthy for felling. Its feet have two toes pointing forward and two pointing backward, and its tail is strong and tensile, suitable for supporting the body when it pecks at the tree bark with its long, sharp beak. Its strong toes with hooked nails enable the bird not only to cling to the tree but also to hop vertically around the tree trunk, and its strong tail supports the body from sliding back. The woodpecker starts at the base of the tree, gradually spiralling up the trunk as it rids the tree thoroughly of worms. The woodpecker also has a long, agile tongue that has many inverted pimples and is covered with a layer of sticky liquid. After the bird has drilled a hole in the bark with its sharp beak, it thrusts in its sticky tongue to suck out larvae and worm eggs. In flight the bird rises and falls as its wings open and close.

The blue-throated barbet (*Megalaima asiatica*) is called the imitation woodpecker, but it feeds mainly on fruits and berries. The bird is very beautiful, its body green, the fore and hind parts of its crown crimson and the throat light blue. It lives in the forests of valleys, hills and plains in Yunnan Province and Guangxi Zhuang Autonomous Region. At dawn the bird begins to busy itself in fruit trees. Usually it moves about singly; even during the breeding season group activities do not last long. The bird sings pleasantly and is easy to rear, so it is likely it will ultimately become a pet bird.

Woodpeckers rarely move in flocks. The holes they drill in tree trunks depend on the strength of each bird. Strong birds with long beaks choose hardwood trees, whereas small, weak birds make holes in soft or rotten tree trunks. The bottom of the hole is usually covered with a layer of wood powder, on which the female lays white eggs. People used to believe that the eggs were white because there was no need for protective coloration, but actually the whiteness makes it easy for the female bird to see the eggs in the dark hole.

Section *VII*

Passeres (Songbirds)

There are about 5,100 species of songbirds in the world, accounting for the greater part of the kingdom of birds. Most are small, but they vary in both body size and appearance. The willow warbler, sunbird, flowerpecker and silver eye are very small, whereas the raven is rather big. Songbirds live in almost all types of environments throughout China — forests, grasslands, hills, deserts, water margins, town and country. Most, however, live in trees or bushes, and a few live on the ground. Songbirds have a complex larynx and voice muscles that make them capable of singing or mimicking. Most are good at building nests. The young are almost naked when hatched and mature late. Songbirds are the most advanced of the birds, appearing late in the course of evolution. Coming at the critical stage of adaptive radiation, they are immensely diversified. Some songbirds are useful to farming and forestry, while most make lovely pets.

The Mongolian skylark (*Melanocorypha mongolica*) sings from dawn till dusk on sunlit plains, boundless grasslands or golden wheat fields. It fills the air with its sweet song, investing the earth with vigour and liveliness. The bird dwells in the northern part of China but winters in east China. It sings all day long, partly for amusement, partly for courting. When the male takes wing, it shoots up almost vertically with all its strength, singing all the while. Then it folds its wings and drops like a stone until very near the ground before soaring again. After several such flights the male and female pair up. There is a clear-cut division of labour between male and female on housekeeping matters. The female is in charge of making their nest in a wheat field or haystack, while the male is responsible for collecting building material. During breeding the female lays two clutches of eggs, each consisting of three to five eggs. Hatching takes fifteen days. The skylark is clever enough to avoid flying directly out of or into its nest. It always takes off or lands some distance from its nest, walking a short distance through thick growth to and from its nest so that no enemy will discover it. Its day-long exertion, flying and singing, makes the bird voracious, so it has to eat many worms, insects and seeds to replenish the energy it has consumed. Thus the bird is helpful in killing field or grassland pests.

The wren (*Troglodytes troglodytes*) is found widely in south and north China. Despite its small size, the male wren sings louder than all birds at dawn. It even sends out a short, beautiful note in the bitter cold of winter. When the breeding season begins, the male wren builds several nests for the female to choose from. The domed nest is roomy enough to allow as many as fifteen young.

The barn swallow (*Hirundo rustica*) continually flaps its wings in flight. Its long tail is forked like open scissors. When the willow bursts into tender green and the peach tree into pink blossoms, the barn swallow returns to China, having crossed the ocean from the tropics. The bird lives in plains, building its nest under the eaves of houses in towns and villages. After the male and female have chosen a nest site, they fetch earth and make mud balls with saliva for the base of the nest. With straw and feathers, they make a nest shaped like half a bowl with a wide opening on top. The inside of the nest is padded with soft feathers and straw. All summer the barn swallow labours twelve hours a day catching insects. On fine days it flies high; when it is overcast and low atmospheric pressure forces insects to fly low, the swallow also flies low. When feeding its young, the barn swallow makes more than five hundred trips a day. Thus a family of swallows may wipe out more than one million insects in summer. "The dark bird comes in midspring and leaves in midautumn," says an ancient Chinese book. In autumn when the cold wind rises and the temperature drops, insects begin to retire into hibernation. The barn swallow sees that food is getting scarce, so in September and October swallows fly south in large flocks. At that time we often see large numbers of swallows resting on electric wires, indicating they are about to begin their long migration to the warm south. The Chinese have loved the swallow since ancient times. The Tang Dynasty poet Li Bai wrote:

Pair after pair of swallows,
What envy the flying pairs evoke.
In jade pavilions they never sleep
alone;
Under golden eaves they never part.

The black-naped oriole (*Oriolus chinensis*) has a yellow body, so it is also called yellow bird in China, but its crown is ringed with black feathers and its wings and tail also have some black feathers. The female is a bit lighter in colour than the male and has a greenish hue. The male sings well and its ringing voice is heard all day. One of the ten scenic spots on West Lake in Hangzhou is called Orioles Singing Amid Waving Willows, and a beautiful pavilion in the Summer Palace in Beijing is named Pavilion for Listening to Orioles.

The oriole is rather shy. It never alights on the ground, but instead hides in the upper branches of trees. Its song is rhythmic and melodic. "Who knows of spring, unless you ask the oriole," wrote the Song Dynasty poet Huang Tingjian (1045 – 1105). The oriole's nest is made of dry grass bound together with spider's web and hangs from on the tip of a tree branch. The parent birds make nearly a hundred trips a day to feed their young, catching harmful forest pests such as weevils and beetles.

The tit (*Parus.*) is a common species in China and there are a large number of varieties. The relatively common great tit (*Parus major*) has a bluish-black cap and a white face that stand out against its surroundings. The bird sings merrily and likes to dwell in orchards on hills and plains. It usually builds its nest in tree holes or walls. If there is no outside intruder, it leads a peaceful life there and rarely moves to another place. The great tit hops and flies from one tree to another to catch insects,

eating a wide variety of pests destructive to fruit trees. When we celebrate a good fruit harvest, we should not forget the tit's contribution. It eats it body weight in insects every day. In winter when the earth is snowbound and insects are hibernating, the great tit still hops in the trees, carefully looking underneath the snow to see whether there are any insects hidden under the bark. When it finds one, it uses its sharp beak to pick it out and devour it. Foresters sometimes make birdboxes to lure great tits, so their forests will be better protected from pests.

The paradise flycatcher (*Terpsiphone paradisi*) resembles the sparrow except for its long tail, which looks like two ribbons when in flight and like waving willow branches when the bird rests on a tree. The bird is mostly white with a metallic black. Its head is green below and brown at the back. Because of its beauty the Chinese also call it "flowering branch." People in ancient China gave this bird as a birthday present, so it was also called "bird of longevity." The flycatcher is a great protector of forests. It keeps its flat beak, barbed on the edge like that of the swallow, wide open to catch insects when in flight, catching the nest during the breeding season, when it needs more nourishment. The bird builds its nest high in a tree and lays three or four eggs at a time. Resident in eastern China, it is seen also in Gansu, Sichuan and Yunnan provinces. The paradise flycatcher is not numerous in the wild, so it must be protected.

The hwamei (*Garrulax canorus*) has been loved by Chinese poets since ancient times. The Song Dynasty poet Ouyang Xiu (1007 – 1072) wrote these lines:

Singing a thousand melodies
Amid flowering trees and bushes;
Singing far better there
Than lonely in a cage.

China, with its many varieties, is

known as the kingdom of hwameis. The hwamei not only sings well but also mimicks other songbirds, making it a favourite pet bird. An ancient Chinese book entitled *Notes on Hwamei* says, "The male is good at singing, and if it sees another male, it starts a fight, but the female is not like this." The bird lives mainly in bushes, usually singly, and sings while hidden amid branches. If frightened, it quickly flies down to the base of the tree and runs for cover. It sings particularly energetically when dusk falls. The bird feeds mainly on insects, especially during the growing season for farm crops. China has 131 of the 287 species of hwamei in the world.

The red-billed leiothrix (*Leiothrix lutea*) is another China specialty. This small, agile bird not only sings lovely tunes but also has lovely plumage, with a yellow throat and olive-green upperparts. Its bill, of course, is red. The bird is prized not only in China but also in many parts of the world. It is generally said that the birds always live in pairs. When one dies, the other dies of heartbreak. Thus people regard the bird as a symbol of love and make it a wedding present. The bird prefers to live in bamboo groves, moving about mainly in the lower branches, but also seeking food in the middle and top strata of trees. It lives in flocks or in mixed communities with other birds, flying out of the valley to higher slopes at sunrise. When it sings, it often stands on the top of a bush, flapping its wings while singing.

The willow warbler (*Phylloscopus*), a tiny bird, lives in trees and bushes, on grassland, in marshes and reed swamps and amid other natural environment. Its voices is clear and high-pitched, sometimes with a tremolo. The bird likes to hop on willow branches. Its plumage is very pretty, olive green all over, except for the eye ring and underparts, which are somewhat yellowish green. It feeds almost entirely on insects

(99.28 percent) and occasionally on spiders and plants. Mostly it eats moths and insect eggs.

A rare species of warbler is the common tailorbird (*Orthotomus sutorius*), found in south and southwest China. When it rests on a branch or hops about, its tail points up. The bird breeds between April and August and constructs a very special nest. It takes one or two big leaves, such as banana, wild rose or grape, and, using plant fibre, such as cotton, silk or fine grass, sews them along the edge into a bag, which it lines on the bottom with plant down or palm fibre, then pads with soft grass, horsehair, wool or cotton. The tailoring of the nest is generally done by the female bird, who pricks the leaves with its bill and sews with plant fibre. Sometimes it anchors the bag to a branch with the leaf stems and grass fibre. The nest, about two metres above-ground, holds three or four tiny eggs — white, light red, light green, blue, light blue or azure with some spots on them. The tailorbird feeds on insects harmful to longan trees, sugarcane and kapok trees.

The sunbird (*Aethopyga*) is the tiniest songbird in China. The yellow-backed sunbird (*Aethopyga siparaja*) weighs no more than five grammes, but the bird is very agile and beautiful with shining plumage —for the male, red back, yellow rump, and long metallic-green tail. The female, however, is plain—greyish yellow underparts and olive green upperparts. The sunbird likes tropical and subtropical forests, particularly flowering trees and bushes. It lives singly, in pairs or small groups, usually the males outnumbering the females. The male is very attractive, its red body brilliant against nature's green backdrop. The bird flies fast and likes to halt in mid-flight by flapping its wings forward. Sometimes it also flaps its wings rhythmically when resting on a branch and sometimes it makes sudden turns in flight. It feeds mainly on

Lark.

Asian paradise flycatcher.

Top to bottom: Minivets, rufous-backed shrike, hwamei, great tit.

Top to bottom: Bohemian waxwing, weaver, sunbird, white-eye, ruby throat, black drongo.

Grackle

Old world oriole.

Red-billed leiothrixes.

nectar by thrusting its long bill into flowers and sucking with its tubelike tongue. It is thus a disseminator of pollen. The perennially flowering coconut palm is one of its haunts.

The silver-eye (*Zosterops*), also called whiteeye, is a small bird almost entirely yellowish green except for a white ring around the eye. The bird breeds in Hebei Province in north China and also in northeastern provinces and winters in southern Yunnan and the Xisha Islands. It lives in willows, fruit trees and other broadleaf trees. In summer the male and female live in pairs. Their food consists mainly of insects. Because the bird is small and has a sweet voice, it is often caged.

Two species of waxwing winter in China. The Bohemian waxwing (*Bombycilla garrulus*) often lives in flocks of dozens or hundreds. It likes to hop on pine branches and leafless twigs but seldom on the ground. In a flock all the birds follow if one takes wing. The bird is a soft pinkish brown with bright sealing-wax red appendages on its secondaries. It eats everything, but mainly fruit. Its young eat insects.

The grackle (*Gracula religiosa*) is black all over with a metallic tint. Two yellow wattles emerge from the back of its head. The bird sings well and, like the parrot, can mimic human speech, so it is loved by people in China. The bird resides in the southern part of Yunnan Province, Guangxi and Hainan Island. Grackles gather in threes and fours in search of food on fruit trees and become particularly active during the breeding season. They live in mixed communities with starlings and mynas in Yunnan Province, singing and hopping on the tops of flowering fruit trees. A caged grackle can be taught simple speech. The bird nests in rotten tree holes or abandoned woodpecker nests. It usually lays eggs in the same hole or one above or below the old

one year after year, so very often two or three pairs are found residing in the same tree.

The magpie and the crow, the commonest birds in China, are resident birds and among the larger songbirds. Unfortunately, they aren't good singers. Superstitious people in old China thought the cry of the crow was a bad omen whereas that of the magpie was a good one, perhaps because the crow's call grates on the ear while the magpie's is pleasant. The crow's black colouring is also related to mourning. To make things worse, witches in the old days talked much about the bad luck brought by crows. The magpie has white splashes on the shoulders, sides and lower breast, and its black feathers are brilliant. Its long tail points up when it's at rest. The magpie likes to sing on trees near houses. It often uses its powerful legs to search for insects on the ground. Three species of magpie reside in China — the common magpie (*Pica pica*), the azure-winged magpie (*Cyanopica cyana*), and the red-billed magpie (*Urocissca erythrorhyncha*) — found extensively in northern China. The red-billed magpie, in the eastern part of the country, has a long tail with transverse black-and-white stripes, a purplish-grey back and white underparts. It flies gracefully and is more prized than its cousins.

Of the crow family's many varieties the most commonly seen are the rook (*Corvus frugilegus*), the thick-billed crow (*Corvus macrorhynchos*) and the collared crow (*Corvus torquatus*). The crow is widely distributed on the plains of China, living near villages and feeding on grass seed and animal carcasses. The crow is solitary by nature and usually lives in pairs, but in the morning and evening crows gather on adjacent trees and crow several times to attract other birds. In winter crows move about in flocks of dozens or over a hundred. A rare species is the yellow-billed chough (*Pyrrhocorax graculus*), which is black all over except for a yellow bill. It lives on the Qinghai-Tibet

Plateau in limited numbers. It prefers high altitudes; Chinese mountaineers have found the bird at 6,900 metres above sea level on Mount Xixiabangma.

The Siberian rubythroat (*Luscinia calliope*) breeds in northern China and winters in southeastern coastal areas. The male is marked by a red throat. The bird's sweet singing with a pleasant tremolo during the day and a low, lyrical tone in the quiet of night is familiar to many. When it rests, the bird often spreads its tail into a fan or erects it almost to touch its head. When it sings, it stays high in a tree or on top of a wall. Because it sings in all four seasons it is also called the "four-happy" bird in China.

The minivet (*Pericrocotus*) is beautiful, particularly when a flock of minivets flies over treetops, because the male minivet is bright red and the female is yellow. The bird is also a natural enemy to forest pests, since it eats insects in the moss layer or on the leaves and branches of trees on Hainan Island and in Guangxi in China. It also catches insects in the air. The bird's call is seldom heard, unless two flocks of minivets meet and sound crisp cries of "*spe — et, spe — et.*"

The shrike (*Lanius*), with nine species in China, has a well-developed beak like that of the eagle — an indication of its fierceness. It feeds on insects and other small birds. When it has more than enough food, it hangs the meat on a branch or thorn and tears it bit by bit. The rufous-backed shrike (*Lanius schach*) raises its head and erects its tail whenever it cries with its powerful voice, but its heroic singing is not very pleasant to the ear.

There are seven species of drongo (*Dicrurus*) in China. Drongoes feed entirely on insects. Most common in China is the black drongo (*Dicrurus macrocercus*), which is glossy black all over with a forked tail. The bird is widely distributed in the eastern part of China. Because it rises very early every day, people also call it the "dawn chicken." It waits on tree tops or electric wire and swoop down on any insect that happens to fly past underneath it. The bird often flies low over water, so it has another name, the "drinking bird." Sometimes it rests on the back of a grazing animal, waiting for insects to be attracted by the animal. Two rare varieties of drongo are the lesser racquet-tailed drongo (*Dicrurus remifer*) and the greater racquet-tailed drongo (*Dicrurus paradisevs*) in south Yunnan and Hainan Island. They earn their names from their long, graceful tail feathers, which look like badminton racquets. The greater racquet-tailed drongo looks like a dancer performing a beautiful dance in the air when it flies with its long black tail feathers waving.

The weaver (*Ploceus*) is limited to the Xishuangbanna region of Yunnan Province. The bird is small and reddish brown with black stripes. Despite its tiny body, the bird is capable of weaving a bottle-shaped nest scores of centimetres long. The nest is hung on a tree branch by the neck of the bottle, sometimes just over a pond. The bird uses soft, tensile plant leaves, first pricking a hole at one end of a leaf, then tearing the leaf into fine shreds from the other end. After tying one end to a tree branch, the bird begins weaving the neck of the nest for several centimetres, then gradually enlarges the diametre to make it hollow. It makes a reinforcing ring at the largest point, the waist, of the nest. Below that point the nest forms a cuplike chamber with the entrance facing downward. To steady it against the wind, the bird sometimes puts mud balls in the nest as a weight. The bird has to fly into the nest from below and cannot stay in the entrance. The nest is built entirely by the male, which starts courting the female the day the nest is finished. During courtship the abler

Bill and foot of a swimming bird.

Bill and foot of a wading bird.

Bill and foot of a pheasant.

Bill and talons of a bird of prey.

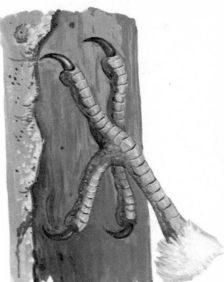

Bill and foot of a climbing bird.

Bill and foot of a pigeon.

Bills and foot of songbirds.

males hang downward from their nests performing stunts and emitting grating sounds to attract females. The less able ones can only make a lot of noise while hanging from their nests. When the female accepts, she enters the nest. Originally it was believed that male and female weavers made their nests together, the female working from inside and the male from outside. Observation showed that to be false.

Chapter Two

Distribution of Birds in China

Thanks to their ability to fly, birds are widely distributed; wherever there are human beings, there are birds. If we take their areas of perennial residence or reproduction as the criterion, there is no species of bird in the world that lives solely in the Palearctic region, but quite a number are peculiar to or mainly distributed in the Palearctic or Nearctic region and are also found in China. The Irenidae family, which is representative of the birds of southern China and peculiar to the Oriental region, and families found mainly in the Oriental region are also found in China. This shows that the regional composition of birds in China is fairly diverse. The distribution of birds in China can be divided into seven regions according to the distribution of endemic, dominant and economic species — Northeast China, North China, Xinjiang-Inner Mongolia, Qinghai-Tibet, Southwest China, Central China and South China. The first four belong to the Palearctic Region and the last three to the Oriental region, as shown in the following chart:

Zoogeographic Region	Zoogeographic Subregion	Region of China
Palearctic	East Asia	Northeast
		North
	Central Asia	Xinjiang-Inner Mongolia
		Qinghai-Tibet
Oriental	Sino-India	Southwest
		Central
		South

Note: Birds in the world may be classified into six zoogeographic regions; the Palearctic, Nearctic, Oriental, Ethiopian, Austrilian and Neotropical. China belongs to the Palearctic and Oriental regions.

1. Northeast China: the northern-most part of China, covering mountain forests and wooded grasslands of the Greater and Lesser Xing'an Mountains and the Changbai Mountains. Forest species, such as divers, the capercaillie and the waxwing, thrive in this region — all typical of the Palearctic. Divers and the capercaillie, especially, are limited to this region for the period of reproduction, although one species of capercaillie is also found in southwest China.

2. North China, including the southern part of Gansu, Shanxi, the loess highlands of Shaanxi, the north China plain and Shandong peninsula. Farming has long reduced the original vegetation cover of broad-leaf forests to grassland, irrigated groves and farmland. Birds peculiar to this region are the brown eared pheasant, the long-tailed pheasant, the Chukor partridge, the red-footed falcon and the azure-winged magpie. Some tropical migrants are also found in this region in summer.

3. The Xinjiang-Inner Mongolia region, including the arid region west of the Greater Xing'an Mountains and north of the Great Wall and the Kunlun Mountains. Animals are scarce in this vast region and birds residing here are only those acclimatized to life in the desert, such as the sandgrouse and the lark. Because of the scarcity of trees some birds nest in holes abandoned by rodents and rabbits. The red-crowned crane, peculiar to northeast China, migrates to marshy tundra in the northeastern part of the region for breeding.

4. The Qinghai-Tibet region: covering the plateau surrounded by the Kunlun, Himalaya and Hengduan mountains. Because of the high altitude, rarified air and frigid climate, plants and animals are scarce, but some species of birds, such as the griffon vulture, are peculiar to the region. All birds in the region are of the alpine variety.

5. Southwest China including the Hengduan Mountains. The perpendicular rise and fall of the topography of the region and the resultant vertical changes in the vegetation, cover have a conspicuous effect on the animal distribution in the region. There are quite a number of bird species peculiar to the region, such as the Chinese copper pheasant, the blood pheasant, the monal and a number of varieties of the hwamei, but there are also some north China species in the northern and higher parts of the region, such as the hazel grouse and the goldcrest. In the lower Hengduan Mountains parrots, sunbirds and partridges can be found. Thus this area represents a transitional zone where the Palearctic and Oriental regions overlap.

6. Central China: covers the Yangtze valley east of the Sichuan basin. The natural vegetation of the region has been gravely damaged and the landscape in the main is that of farmland. Thanks to other advantageous natural conditions, however, the region still boasts quite a number of species of birds, such as the golden pheasant, the white-necked long-tailed pheasant and the red-billed leiothrix. The central China region bears features of both the north and the south. Species of the Palearctic region reaching here include the azure-winged magpie and the Penduline tit. Even more southern species reach the region, such as the minivet, drongo, hwamei and flower-pecker.

7. South China: the tropical location of the region favours the multiplication of birds. This region covers the southern parts of Yunnan, Guangxi, Guangdong and Fujian, Taiwan, Hainan Island and the archipelago in the South China Sea. The region consists mainly of tropical monsoon forest, so there are many tropical species, such as parrots, hornbills, leafbirds and sunbirds. Bluebirds are endemic birds peculiar to the Oriental region. In addition,

there are rare species, such as the green peafowl, the red jungletfowl and the Red-footed booby.

Birds of Taiwan and Hainan Island are similar to those on the mainland of China. Any difference is in the varieties. There are only a few endemic species, such as the Hainan hill partridge, on Hainan Island and very few in Taiwan. This shows that the two islands have not been separated from the mainland long. Taiwan also has some birds of the Palearctic region, such as the goldcrest (*Regulus regulus*), an indication of the island's connection with the northern animal realms of the mainland, whereas no birds of the Palearctic region are found on Hainan Island.

Divers, capercaillies, waxwings, gold-crests and crossbills of northeast China, north China, Xinjiang-Inner Mongolia and Qinghai-Tibet regions all belong to the Palearctic region. Birds such as parrots, minivets, drongos, hwameis, sunbirds and leafbirds, living in southwest,

central and south China, retain characteristics of the Oriental region and other tropical animal regions:

The demarcation line between the Palearctic and Oriental regions may run along the Himalayas, the mountains and valleys of the Hengduan Mountains and the uneven edge of the grassland plateau of Qinghai and Tibet to the Min Mountains in northern Sichuan and the Qinling Mountains in Shaanxi, then eastward along the Funiu Mountains and the Huai River to north of the Yangtze River estuary. It is difficult to mark a division line because terrains overlap to varying degrees in these regions. The north-south alignment of the Hengduan Mountains provides channels for north-south exchange in southwest China, so species of the Palearctic and Oriental regions tend to mingle. That is why there is a vast transitional area in both the mountainous areas of the western part of the country and the coastal areas of the eastern part.

Migration Routes of Chinese Migratory Birds

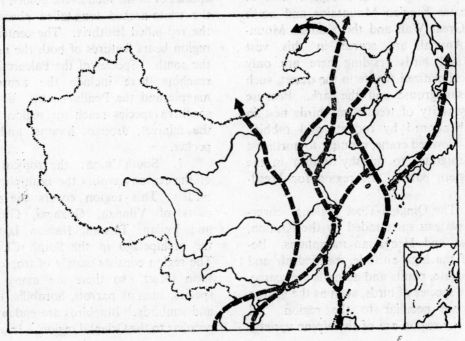

Chapter Three

Migration

The bird population in any region changes during the year as birds come and go. This phenomenon, the result of bird migration, has long been noted by man. *Lu's Almanac*, written in the Warring States Period (475 – 221 B.C.), says, "The wild geese go north early in spring," and "the wild geese come south early in autumn." The *Book of Rites*, written in the late Han Dynasty (206 B.C.-A.D. 220), in the chapter on seasons says, "In midspring peach trees begin blossoming and swallows and cuckoos sing."

Birds can be classified into different categories according to their migrating habits. Those that stay in one place all the year round, such as the magpie and sparrow, are called residents; resident birds that wander in search of food, for instance, in wooded hills in summer and on plains in winter, such as the woodpecker and the turtledove, are called wanderers; birds that migrate to different places according to the change of seasons are called migrants. Those that come in spring and summer to build nests and reproduce are called summer migrants; those that come to pass the winter are called winter migrants. Migrant birds that stray from their migration routes and get lost because of a gale, a sudden change of weather or other accident are called stragglers. For example, we occasionally see sandhill cranes in the coastal area of Jiangsu Province and Egyptian geese over Beijing.

Birds generally migrate twice a year,

once in spring and once in autumn. In spring they move from their wintering place to breeding place and vice versa in autumn. The time varies, some birds going earlier, some later. The time may vary even among birds of the same species, a few setting out earlier and the majority following. Often the male and the female do not migrate at the same time. The earlier spring migrants usually leave later in autumn, so they stay at their breeding place longer than others. The later spring migrants leave earlier in autumn, so they stay a shorter time. Birds often follow an order of age or sex during migration. The skylark and bush robin fly in the order of young first, then adult female, then adult male, whereas the older cuckoos and shrikes always precede the younger.

The bigger birds keep to certain formations during flight, such as the straight line or V of cranes and wild geese. Birds of medium size, such as the starling (*Sturnus*), fly in a cluster. Small birds, such as the brambling (*Fringilla montfringilla*), are scattered during migration. Birds of prey, however, keep a great distance from one another; each flies alone. Ducks fly in family groups. Some birds fly only in flocks of the same species, whereas others fly with birds of other species. Most birds fly at night. Small birds specially rest and look for food during the day and avoid attacks by birds of prey by flying at night. Some ducks fly at night over land but during the day over water. Daytime migrants are mostly big birds.

Birds generally fly very fast, but during migration flight is not necessarily fast, some birds ranging from twenty to fifty kilometres a day. They fly faster in spring than in autumn. The height of their flight during migration also varies a great deal. It is a mistaken conception that birds fly very high in migration. Only a few species fly above a thousand metres; the majority at a height of several hundred metres. The small birds fly below a hundred metres or even close to the ground. They fly higher on a fine day and lower when it is cloudy or windy. We rarely see birds flying above the clouds in migration, thus it is believed that birds like to keep the ground in sight during flight. Moreover, migrant birds fly along fixed routes, along definite rivers, coastlines, mountain ranges or other topographical features. Occasionally their spring routes differ from their autumn routes, depending on weather and nutrition. There are two known migration routes for birds in China. One is along the coastline to the Yangtze valley, where many birds go up the river to the hinterland, while others continue northward along the coastline to the Shandong peninsula and Hebei Province or cross Bohai Bay to reach the east Liaoning peninsula. The other route is from Taiwan via Japan and Korea to reach northeast China, where some birds continue northward to Sakhalin, then across the sea to Siberia.

Take Shanghai, for example. There are 282 species of birds in the Shanghai area, including 237 migrants. Most summer migrants arrive in April and May, though egrets and barn swallows arrive in early and mid March. Orioles and cuckoos come next, arriving in mid April. Paradise flycatchers and turtledoves bring up the rear, arriving in mid May. In August and September barn swallows and others set off for the south, while turtledoves and some others leave as late as mid October. The winter migrants generally come to Shanghai in October and leave in March and April of the next year. Some stay even longer, arriving in early October and leaving in mid May of the next year. Migrants passing over Shanghai generally fly by between March and May in spring and September and October in autumn. There are two ways to observe the migration of birds: by direct observation in open fields and by banding. Banding makes it possible to record migration routes, the sequence of birds in migration, the time and speed of flight and even the life span of the birds. Such records provide scientific data for ornithological study.

Chapter Four

Reproduction

Most birds occupy a territory when they start building their nests. The size varies according to the species and even among birds of the same species. Generally, the smaller birds have smaller territory, whereas birds of prey have a much larger territory. Birds with different eating habits, such as ones that feed on worms and ones that feed on grass seed, do not interfere with each other although their territories overlap. As a rule, the male bird arrives at the breeding place earlier than the female and immediately starts looking for its territory. When it has found one, it perches on a prominent point and begins to call, as if saying, "I'm going to live here! I'm going to live here!" The male birds in adjacent territories respond. Seizing territory is important for finding food. However, this is not so vital for birds like the swift, seagull and crow, which build nests in flocks, because they have rich food resources to meet the needs of the parent birds and the fledgelings and they can fly far to find food.

The eagle, the red footed falcon and other birds of prey may extend their territory to several or even dozens of square kilometres, whereas the great tit's territory covers only forty to two hundred square metres. The territory of the warbler, robin and other small birds is even smaller, covering less than a hundred square metres. The territory of some birds living in flocks, such as some sea birds living on seaside cliffs, may be just one or two square metres for each bird or merely a bill's length away. Naturally, such territory is meant for mating and resting, not for food collecting. Establishing territory allows pairs to maintain a distance and reduce outside disturbance to the couple's oestrus, mating and nursing the young. The sexes among the wild ducks, for example, are not in proportion. When males outnumber females, that poses a threat to the already paired couples, so the female chooses a spouse in the wintering place and the couple fly to the breeding place. Territories also facilitate an even distribution of birds in the breeding area, prerenting overcrowding. Birds need a constant food supply as a result of their high metabolism. This calls for a continuous supply of food. Fledgelings especially need to be fed a hundred or hundreds of times a day. This naturally calls for a fixed place to give a steady supply of food. Sometimes parents find the food supply within their territory inadequate for feeding their young and they have to seek elsewhere. However, occasionally a male bird is found to have slackened its vigilance and allowed other birds to seek food in its territory during the period of nursing its young. This may be attributed to a decrease of the male hormone. Birds generally show a strong nostalgia for their former territories; about 80 percent return to a place within ten kilometres of their old territory. About 14 percent are in the neighbourhood of 10 kilometres from their old territory. Only a few species establish an entirely new territory.

The male bird generally gets in heat earlier than the female and their oestrus is affected by weather and food. A sudden worsening of the weather may affect or even suppress the reproductive ability of birds. Since breeding expends a great deal of the birds energy, they can lay eggs only under normal conditions. Therefore changes in latitude and amount of sunshine cause differences in reproduction time.

The singing of birds is their principal way of courtship. The male often perches on a branch and sings continually. The song of the hwamei and leiothrix during the breeding period is very sweet, and the magpie robin and thrush have rich, beautiful melodies, sometimes like the sound of a flute from a distance. Some male birds court the female by showing off their beautiful plumage, notably the peacock. When two peacocks are courting a peahen, they dance amid flowers and trees, displaying their plumage to the full, as if they were having a beauty contest. The long feathers on each side of the lyrebird's tail make it look very much like a lyre when the bird is in heat and erects the tail. At other times the male lyrebird's tail just trails behind. Still other male birds have special ways of courting. When in heat, the wild goose stretches its neck downward; the male pintail spreads its tail feathers and lowers itself in the air, causing the thin tail to wave slightly while the bird cries out. When the

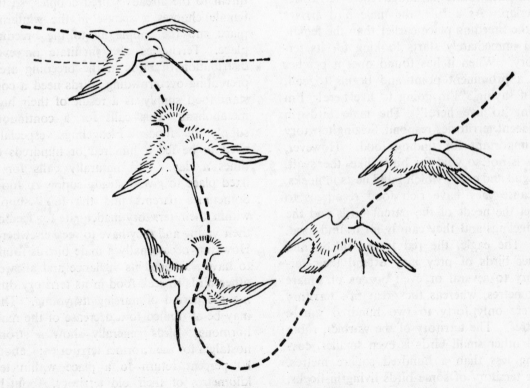

A male pintail in courtship in flight

Black grouses in courtship

short-tailed albatross is in heat, it dashes its body against waves, leaving behind a long trail of foam. The paradise bird in heat stretches out its secondary wings, which are ordinarily hidden. At this time, the two longest tail feathers open and close. Sometimes the bird drops dozens of metres from the treetop as silently as a falling leaf. When it almost touches the ground, it flaps its wings, makes a sudden turn and shoots into the sky. Sometimes dozens of male paradise birds gather and dance in trees with their golden tail feathers spread, looking like golden clouds.

Birds such as the common pheasant and the capercaillie, whose two sexes have different colouring, have distinctive courtship habits that last very long. When in heat, the black grouse of northeast China gather in forest clearings. The male runs about with its wings raised and tail feathers spread. The males often feud over a female, the female watching nonchalantly from the edge of the forest or in the bushes. Courtship

among birds with similar plumage is not conspicuous. The male willow warbler merely repeatedly spreads its tail into a fan and calls while the female perches on a tree branch and responds. When a male and female grebe meet, they just keep nodding to each other.

Most birds practise monogamy. Eagles, falcons, cranes, wild geese, swans and many other birds keep their spouses for many years and, some say, if one spouse dies, the other remains single the rest of its life. Nevertheless, most birds mate only during the breeding period. After that they part. Some relationships are for only a few hours or even a few minutes.

After a territory is chosen, the birds begin building their nests. Generally they build their nests in sheltered places, some in treetops, some hanging from branches, some hidden in thick grass, some in holes and some on water. The nest serves as a cradle. Adults enter the nest only to lay eggs and nurse their young. They seek

— 45 —

Grebes in courtship

food in forest or field during the day and sleep in trees or bushes at night.

Different birds nest at different times. Vultures living on Tibetan mountains start building their nests when the fields are still blanketed with snow. This is because vulture fledgelings take a long time to grow up. The young are hatched in April and remain with the parents through September. In the first few months after the young are hatched, melting snows reveal the carcasses of dead animals, thus providing an ample supply of food. Crossbills breed in winter because there are abundant supplies of conifer seeds in winter. The young are hatched just as winter is turning to spring and the pine cones are opening up. This makes it easy for young crossbills to find food. Sparrow hawks build their nests later than others. When the young sparrow hawks are hatched, the young bramblings are leaving the nest. Therefore there is no conflict, although the fledgelings of both birds feed on the same food.

Usually the female is in charge of nest building. It is almost solely the female tit's business to build the nest while the male tit just stands by and "cheers" her on. Male and female of some birds, such as the barn swallow, oriole, and kingfisher, work together to make their nests. In a few species, for instance, the weaver and the grasshopper warbler (*Locustella naevia*), nest building is entirely or mainly the male's task. The birds build quickly. In fine weather it takes only four or five days to complete the work. In the tropics some birds start building at dawn and stop working when the sun is high.

The nest is used first of all to hold eggs. Without a nest it would be impossible for some birds to lay eggs high aboveground. Many water birds, such as the swan and grebe, are capable of making nests that float on water. Secondly, the nest provides the optimum temperature for hatching, shelters eggs and young from bad weather, and protects the nursing parent from enemy attack. Furthermore, the nest holds all the eggs together, so that they all get warmth from the female bird during hatching. Finally, the nest is where the parents feed their young.

Some primitive birds, such as the ostrich

and brown kiwi (*Apteryx australis*), do not have obvious nests. The floating nests built by some waterfowl are relatively primitive too. The little grebe just bends the tips of reeds to the water and joins them together. Some birds tie their nests to tree branches that touch the water. In this way the nests rise and fall with the surface of the water.

A shallow nest is simply a depression in the ground. The sandpiper, for instance, digs a shallow nest in the dry leaves at the base of bushes. The nightingale usually lays its eggs beneath conifer needles, fallen leaves or rotten wood and makes a small, shallow nest in the course of hatching.

A burrow nest is one dug into a riverbank overgrown with bushes or covered by reeds or into a sandy ridgy in a field by a kingfisher or other bird. The burrow is horizontal and expands into a nest chamber. Some burrows rise a bit towards the end. The entrance is usually covered by hanging roots or grass. Bee-eaters (*Merops.*) dig tunnels together in hillside tombs. The round tunnel, usually 60 centimetres long, gets bigger towards the end to form a nest chamber. On deserts and grasslands in China birds and rodents often share burrow homes. The horned lark (*Eremophila alpestris*) shares its home with the ground squirrel, snow hare or pika. Actually they do not share their homes, because the bird only makes use of the burrow abandoned by the rodent or takes a part of it. This may be attributed to the lack of trees in desert and grassland regions.

The hole nest is a natural hole in a tree that birds such as the hornbill, hoopoe, parrot and woodpecker use. Mandarin

Grebe's floating nest

Kingfisher's burrow nest

ducks also usually nest in treeholes. The height of the hole varies a great deal, some holes being as high as ten metres aboveground. The birds put dry straw or grass on the bottom of the hole and pad it with down from the breast or abdomen of the parent bird. The woodpecker makes its own hole in a tree with its sharp, strong beak. Sometimes it chisels several holes before it is satisfied. The hoopoe pads its hole with straw, leaves and small twigs, but it does not keep it clean, so the hole nest of the hoopoe invariably stinks.

The platform nest of the turtledove is made of twigs, usually on a few horizontal branches. The nest is so crude that one can see the eggs from below, as if it were built solely to hold the eggs. Crude as it is, it can hold both parents and young. The magpie's nest looks like a bundle of twigs, but the twigs are neatly laid with the outer layer consisting of thicker twigs and the inner layer of thinner ones. Straw and mud hold them together, and the nest is covered.

For a mud nest the barn swallow first chooses a site, then takes mud from the field in its bill, shaping each billful into a ball and mixing the mud balls with straw and feathers to shape them into a nest. The

Hornbill's hole nest

nest looks like a halfbowl with the upper side open. Inside there is a matting of feathers and soft straw. The red-rumped swallow is more skillful than the barn swallow. It makes a mud nest the shape of half a vase on a wall. The opening is at the bottleneck and the chamber in the larger lower part. The inside is padded with straw, rags and feathers.

A hanging nest is like a cradle hanging in the air. It is made of bast fibre, wastepaper or cotton and can be taken as a sort of woven nest. Most hanging nests hang from a fork in the branches of trees or bamboo and dangle in the air. The weaver makes its nest near the tip of a branch or where the leaves are thin or on a branch that reaches out over a pond. The nest is woven of grass stems and blades, fibre from willow bark or other tender green plants.

A tailored nest is also complicated. It is made by sewing together two broad leaves, such as those of banana or wild rose. The inside is then padded with straw and other soft material. The nest is usually slanted to prevent rain from getting in. This is indeed highly sophisticated in the birds' kingdom. Besides the tailorbird the fantailed warbler has this habit.

— 49 —

A woodpecker's tree hole

a bird by investigating the type of nest the bird makes.

Atmospheric temperature and food have much to do with egg laying. Since egg laying consumes much energy, the number of eggs per brood is greater in a year with favourable weather than in a year with bad weather. The ostrich lays the biggest egg — 15 centimetres long and 12 centimetres wide, 1.5 kilograms in weight. One ostrich egg equals the total weight of twenty to thirty chicken eggs. The smallest egg is the bee-eater's, which is not bigger than a bean. The eggs of smaller birds are relatively bigger than those of bigger birds, and precocial birds lay bigger eggs than altricial birds. Most eggs are oval, but some are round, such as those of the woodpecker and the blue hill pigeon; some are in the shape of snails, such as those of the auks; some are cylinder shaped, such as the eggs of the sandgrouse, and some are coneshaped, such as those of the sandpiper. Eggs laid in basketlike nests are generally round so that they can be gathered together for the female bird to hatch. Auk eggs, laid on coastal cliffs, are particularly long; the eggs just spin when there is a gale, and there is no danger of their being blown out to sea.

Bird eggs vary in colour. The most primitive eggs, like those of reptiles, are white. The eggs of the woodpecker and kingfisher are white because the nests of these birds are in either tree holes or burrows, where no protective colouring is required. The different colours and patterns of many birds' eggs make the eggs fit in with their surroundings, serving as camouflage against the enemy. For example, the eggs of seagulls have light brown spots resembling beach sand. The eggs of reed warblers are green and white, making them difficult to distinguish from the surrounding reeds. The patterns on the eggs are formed in the course of going through the Fallopian tubes.

An edible nest is made by the edible-nest swiftlet (*Collocalia inexpectata*), which lives in Southeast Asia and makes its nest on coastal cliffs with its saliva. The bird spends a month or so constructing a nest. Its gluelike saliva hardens until it is translucently white. Soaked in water, it expands and softens. Bird's-nest soup is a delicacy in China and is believed to be very nutritious.

Nests provide information about the habits and distribution of birds. Scientists can also judge the degree of evolution of

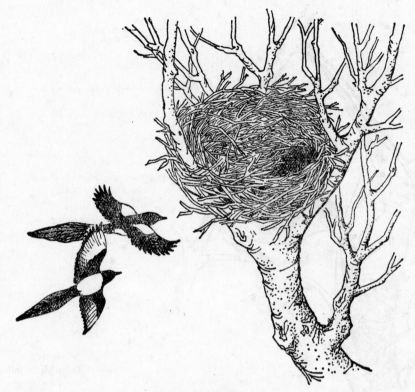

Magpie's platform nest

Barn swallow's mud nest

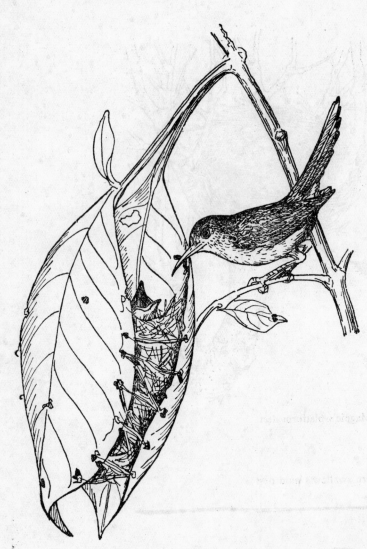

Weaver's hanging nest

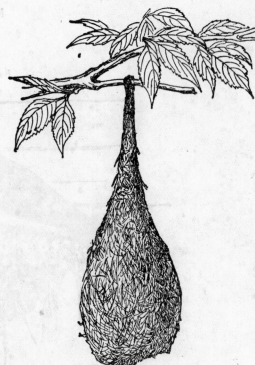

Tailorbird's tailored nest

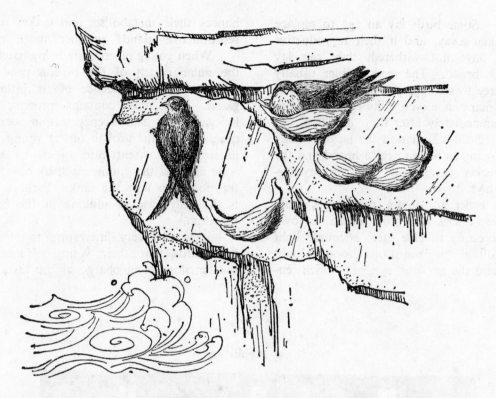

Swiftlet's edible nest

When the egg pauses in the tube, the colour secretion in the tube causes spots on the egg; when the egg moves, the secretion causes stripes or cloud shapes. The eggs of egrets and hwamei are pure blue, those of the grey bushchat (*Saxicola ferrea*) jade green. Few birds have red eggs, but those of the red-whiskered bulbul (*Pycnonotus jocosus*) are pink.

The number of eggs in each brood also varies greatly. The seagull, inhabiting cliffs on solitary islands, lays one egg because there is no fear of outside interference. Divers, pigeons and eagles lay two eggs. Most subtropical songbirds, such as the swallow, the hwamei, the flycatcher and the sparrow, lay three to five eggs. Birds that eat worms, such as the tit and the treecreeper, lay six to ten eggs. Pheasants and wild ducks lay more than ten eggs,

because their eggs, laid on the ground, are more vulnerable to enemy attack. Domestic fowl, such as chickens and ducks, can lay more than a hundred or even two hundred eggs a year.

The number of eggs per brood also varies with the season. An investigation of 1,800 great tit nests showed that the early broods (from April 4 to April 12) averaged 10.3 eggs per brood and the late broods (from June 4 to June 14) averaged 7.4 eggs. This shows that the number of eggs per brood decreases with the advance of the breeding season. The number of eggs per brood for birds of prey varies even with different years. Generally it has much to do with the number of rodents available for birds of prey each year. Many birds lay more than one brood a year. For instance, sparrows lay two or three broods a year. Some birds lay an egg to replace one taken away, and if their reproductive glands have not withered, they can lay another brood. The reed warbler usually lays three to six eggs per brood, but it can lay as many as eleven if its eggs are taken away immediately after they are laid. By such artificial stimulation the jackdaw may lay as many as fifteen eggs a brood and the woodpecker Seventy-one eggs in seventy-three days.

In order to obtain more eggs from chickens, ducks and other domestic fowl, it is necessary to give them adequate light in addition to nutritious food. Light stimulates the nervous system, which en-hances their metabolism and makes their reproductive glands produce more eggs.

When young pigeons are being hatched, the gular pouch of the pigeon produces milk under the influence of its pituitary gland. This milk contains protein, fat, inorganic salt, starch enzyme and sucrose, necessary for the growth of the young. In nursing, the parent bird opens its beak wide and lets the young reach its beak into the pouch to take the milk. Perhaps this is the only case of milking in the birds' kingdom.

It is also very interesting to observe how birds rear their young. Generally, the females are in charge of the task and

Shapes of birds' eggs

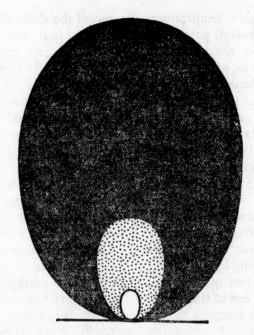

Sizes of birds' eggs

the males just "stand guard," sometimes also bringing food to the female. In quite few species, such as pigeons and woodpeckers, male and female rear their young jointly, but this is rather primitive. For a few species, such as the painted snipe (*Rostratula benghalensis*), rearing of the young is the task of the male. Generally, if the feathers of the two sexes are similar, both male and female take up the brooding. If the two sexes have vastly different plumage, it is usually the sex with plainer feathers that broods. The black male ostrich broods at night, while the brown female broods in the daytime. This arrangement renders some protection to the parent birds. Some birds do not hatch their eggs. The cuckoo, for instance, lays eggs in other birds' nests and lets other birds do the hatching. The megapode has a peculiar way of hatching. It collects plant matter to fill its nest, and with the warmth of the sunshine and the plant fermentation its eggs are hatched.

The time of beginning to hatch varies as well. The eagle, owl and swift begin brooding after the first egg is laid, so their young are of varying size. Most small birds and waders start brooding only after all the eggs are laid, so that they are all hatched at about the same time. This makes nursing much easier. The time needed for the eggs to hatch is different for different birds. The eggs of small birds generally need thirteen to fifteen days; those of medium-size birds, three to four weeks, and those of big birds, even longer. The time is in proportion to the size of the egg. But there are a few exceptions. An ostrich egg weighs 1,500 grams and a booby egg weighs 102 grams, but both take forty-two days to hatch. Brooding means to give the eggs warmth. In brooding the birds shed their down from those parts in contact with the eggs; such patches are called brood patches. The capillaries in the brood patches are well developed, so that the skin of these parts produces much higher temperature. The mechanism of the brood patches is controlled by hormones in the body.

When grebes and ducks want to leave their nests momentarily during the brooding period, they often cover their nests with down and reeds. When an enemy draws near, birds that build nests cling closely to their nests. Birds that lay eggs on the ground without obvious nests quietly leave the spot, then take off so the enemy will not easily discover their nestlings. When the sandpiper finds an enemy approaching, it makes all sorts of manoeuvres, one moment taking off, the next moment landing, then hopping or walking or calling loudly, trying its best to divert the attention of its enemy from its nest. Toward the end of the brooding period a horny growth forms at the tip of the embryo in the egg with which the young breaks the shell. Once the young emerges from the shell, the growth disappears. It takes different amounts of time for the young to get out of the shell. The woodpecker needs five to ten hours to break

out of the shell, whereas the albatross needs one to four days.

Birds can be classified into precocial and altricial types. The young of early maturing birds are called nidifugous. Their eyes and ears are already open at time of hatching, and their bodies are covered with a thick down. When the down dries, they can follow the parent birds in search of food. Birds of this category mostly live on the ground or water, such as quails, cranes, wild geese and ducks. The young of late maturing birds are called nidicolous. At time of hatching their eyes and ears are not open and their bodies have little or no down. They cannot walk. The nidicolous young have to stay in the nest for a long time and be nursed by their parents. When they have grown big enough to fly, their parents teach them how to obtain food. The more advanced birds, such as swallows and sparrows, are late maturing. There are also a few species in the transitional stage between precocial and altricial types. The young of the

Younglings of early maturing (*left*) and late maturing birds

gull, for instance, are covered with a layer of down and can walk right after hatching. Morphologically, they belong to the early maturing type, but since they stay in their nests and are fed by their parents for some time, they also belong to the late maturing type. The inside of the bills of the young of many late maturing birds is an especially bright red or yellow. This stimulates the parents to feed their young. A parent will not feed its fledgeling if it does not open its bill. Some parts of the young bird grow fast. The bill and the tarsometatarsus, for instance, have grown to their full length by the time the bird leaves the nest, but the wings and tail continue to grow for some time afterward.

The behaviour of birds is instinctive. For example, when sparrow hawks nurse their young, the female never leaves the nest. It is up to the male to fetch food, which it gives to the female. The female tears the bigger pieces of food into bits to feed its young one by one. If the female dies, the male just throws the food into the nest without tearing it into pieces, so if the young birds are too small to tear the meat themselves, they die of hunger. The petrel is another case. If its eggs are taken away and replaced with potatoes, the female petrel broods over them all the same. Nursing the young is a reflex.

It is really a sight when birds feed their young. As the parents approach the nest, the young birds stretch their necks and open their bills as wide as possible. Some young birds also call loudly as if to say they are hungry. Some parents can feed all their young with one trip, but others make many trips, feeding one fledgeling on each trip, so it is a taxing task to feed the young. Many birds lose weight during the breeding season. Insectivorous birds feed their young by putting worms directly into the mouths of the young. Carnivorous birds, such as the falcon and eagle, capture rodents and other small animals and tear the meat into small pieces before feeding their young. Fish eaters, such as the pelican and cormorant, carry fish in their gular pouch and open their bills so their young can reach into their throats and take out the fish. The nightjar and green woodpecker swallow the insects they catch, then put their beaks into the beaks of their young and spit out the food.

The parental birds are busy feeding their young during the nursing period. Some birds, such as the oriole and great tit, make a hundred trips a day to fetch food for their young, and the woodpecker makes a hundred twenty trips daily. Once 281 insects were found in the mouth of a nursing swift, including mosquitoes, flies, gadflies and caterpillars. In order to feed their young, some birds work sixteen to nineteen hours a day. In places where the day is long they may work over twenty hours a day.

In the first few days after leaving the nest, the young birds still live with their parents, who continue to feed them. When they can live on their own, they leave their parents. Birds generally have amazing appetites and the young being fed by their parents have even greater appetites. For example, the amount of food a great tit eats weighs as much as its own body. The cuckoo may catch a hundred insects an hour, and a swift may eat two hundred fifty thousand mosquitoes, flies and aphides in a summer. A young pratincole can eat ninety locusts in one day. Thus many birds are valuable in getting rid of pests. Without birds and other natural enemies of insect pests our planet would have been destroyed by the pests.

When the young are still in the nest, their feathers are plain. When they have their full plumage, they begin to learn to fly. A young bird that has just learned to fly is not afraid of human beings. Before they start their independent life, the young birds have to receive some training from their parents, such as where to find food. However, flying is the most important thing. Young birds invariably are timid when they first learn to fly. The parents use every means to get them to try their wings. Sometimes the last nestling is still afraid to leave when all the rest have flown, and the parents give it individual teaching. The parent may even carry a particularly tasty worm in its bill and perch on a nearby branch to lure the timid young bird to take wing. Tantalized by the food, the young forgets its fear and takes off. When the adult birds teach their young to fly, the young birds usually stand in a row on a branch and watch closely as their parents circle overhead. The parents call loudly while showing their young how to fly. At first the young can only leap from one branch to another, then take a long rest. After some time they fly a little farther. Soon the young birds join their parents until they tire. They

practise like this for days in succession and will subsequently be able to fly well. By then they have graduated in the art of flight.

Sometimes in learning to fly a young bird misses the branch and falls to the ground. If threatened by an enemy, the mother bird feins being injured and also drops to the ground, crying loudly to divert the enemy's attention. Sometimes the parent carries its young away. The ruddy shelduck, for instance, carries its young on its back to flee an enemy. Birds that flock together during the breeding period often take concerted action in warding off enemy attacks. Some parents take their young along to fly and feed. The swallow often takes its young to practise gliding in search of flies and mosquitoes. The owl often catches small rats before the eyes of its young, then lets the young do the same. After some time the parents leave their young on their own. At first, the young birds cry for food when they feel hungry, but they have to get food themselves since their parents are not on

Young birds watching the parent birds

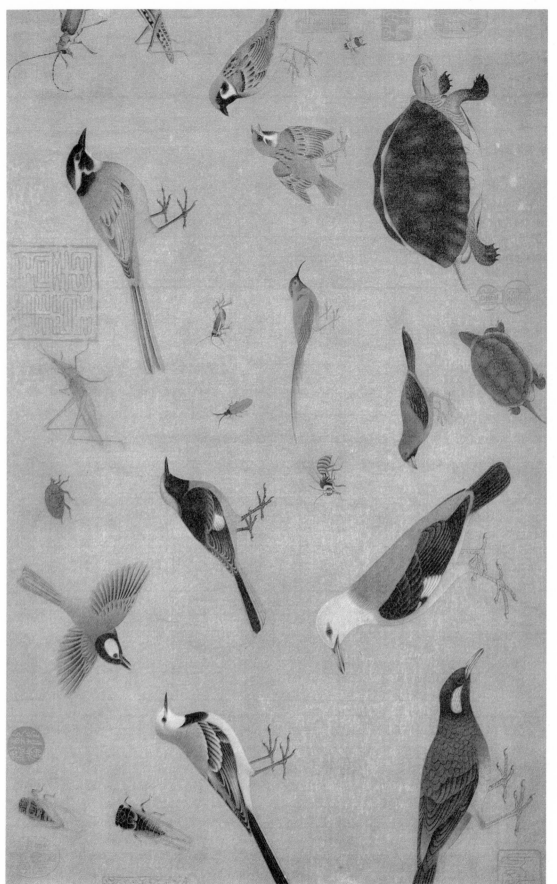

Rare Birds by the Five Dynasties painter Huang Quan (903-965).

Cranes and Bamboo by Bian Wenjin (1403-1423) of the Ming Dynasty.

Swan Geese on a Snow-Covered Bank by Lu Ji (1477-?) of the Ming Dynasty.

Two Birds amid Peonies by Yu Sheng of the Qing Dynasty (1644-1911).

hand. Some songbirds teach their young to sing by first singing a few notes, then pausing to let the young repeat. It seems young birds, like human babies, have to go through a period of learning to speak.

Natural and social phenomena find expression in myths, poems and other literary forms. Birds of all descriptions are related in a thousand and one ways with mythology, poetry and other literary forms.

When social productive forces were very low, man had a poor knowledge of the natural phenomena around him, and that included his knowledge of birds, so man resorted to the primitive literary form of mythology to express his understanding of birds and his desire to use and control birds. A large number of legends related to birds have been handed down from generation to generation in China.

Chapter Five
Birds and the Arts

Natural and social phenomena find expression in myths, poems and other literary forms. Birds of all descriptions are related in a thousand and one ways with mythology, poetry and other literary forms.

When social productive forces were very low, man had a poor knowledge of the natural phenomena around him, and this included his knowledge of birds, so man resorted to the primitive literary form of mythology to express his understanding of birds and his desire to use and control birds. A large number of legends related to birds have been handed down from generation to generation in China.

In Chinese mythology fairies are often accompanied by cranes, presumably because of the graceful, carefree air of this lovely white creature. In some legends the red crowned crane is described as having a very long life. Because the pine tree is a long-lived plants, the pine and the crane became a motif of longevity in traditional Chinese paintings. Actually it is unnatural to put the crane and the pine together since the crane is a wading bird, living on marshland. It does, however, live for fifty to sixty years.

There are quite a number of legends about the cuckoo in China too. *Pi Ya*, a book on birds and beasts written by a Song Dynasty scholar, says, "The cuckoo cries bitterly, shedding blood incessantly."

The Tang Dynasty poet Luo Ye in his poem "Hearing the Cuckoo Crying" wrote:

Why are you crying with eyes bleeding;
Still for the fall of Shu you mourn?
O'er moonlit hills the east wind grieving,
A sleepless heart groans.

Ancient people took the red colour around the beak of the cuckoo for blood and thought that the cuckoo cried so bitterly that it shed blood instead of tears.

The Chinese love mandarin ducks, in literary works the symbol of love and friendship. In olden times many things were named after mandarin ducks. There were mandarin duck quilts in the Han Dynasty (206 B.C.-A.D. 220) as well as during the Five Dynasties period (907-960). Pairs of tiles were called mandarin duck tiles. Even in *Shi Yi Ji* (*Untold Stories Gleaned*), written by Wang Jia of the Eastern Jin Dynasty (317-420), the mandarin ducks were treated as fairies. In the mythological opera *A Marriage with the Seventh Fairy* a devoted couple is compared to mandarin ducks, for mandarin ducks, like most wild geese and other ducks, are monogamous and their relationships may last many years. Some people believe that after one mandarin duck dies, its spouse will live singly until death. However, this belief lacks adequate proof. Mandarin ducks migrate to the Changbai Mountains in northeast China in April, and in June, when the female walks its young along the willow-sheltered river-bank, the male is seen alone moving about in a willow grove. This proves that the belief that a mandarin duck couple never parts is mistaken.

Many ancient Chinese poems speak of birds, their habits, migration and their routes of migration. In *Shi Jing* (the *Book of Odes*), which is a collection of poems written in the period from the Western Zhou (11th century B.C.-771 B.C.) to the Spring and Autumn Period (770-476 B.C.), there is a poem describing the calls of wading birds on a small isle in the middle of a river. Accomplished poets of the Tang Dynasty, such as Li Bai, Du Fu and Bai Juyi, all described birds and their habits in their poems. Li Bai wrote, " . . . the cuckoo cried . . . . in the moonlit night, the hills were filled with sorrow." Among Du Fu's poems are lines like these: "Playful butterflies linger here and there; carefree nightingales sing intermittently." "The swallows come and go in the eaves; the ducks kiss and nestle on the water." "The courtyard of winding corridors is so quiet, the swimming ducks and flying egrets so carefee."

The poet began his wandering life at the age of twenty. He spent much time with his friend, Su Yuanming, admiring birds and beasts and discussing poems. He therefore had an intimate knowledge of the life of birds.

For the brilliance of their plumage and their beautiful shapes birds have always been a pet subject for Chinese painters. In China paintings of birds and flowers have always been an important component of the fine arts since ancient times. The bird-and-flower painters formed a separate school of their own during the Tang Dynasty (618-907) and paintings with birds and flowers as subjects thrived during the Song Dynasty (960-1279). Painter Huang Quan of the Five Dynasties (907-960) was acclaimed for his paintings of birds. He learned from nature, sketching outdoors, and made friends with birds. A legend illustrates Huang Quan's superb technique in painting lifelike birds. Once the king of the state of Shu received some cranes as a present, and the king ordered the painter to paint some cranes on the walls of his palace. When the mural was finished, the painted cranes were so lifelike that the real cranes were attracted to them. Another time the king ordered Huang Quan to paint rabbits, pheasants, and sparrows in four seasons on the walls of his new hall. When the painting was finished, an eagle mistook it for real.

Birds are pretty and their movements graceful. The way tits and orioles take firm grip of branches, parrots grasp twigs in their strong beaks, woodpeckers cling to the bark of trees and hop up the trunk, golden pheasants and silver pheasants look for food on the ground and geese and ducks swim on the water-all these activities arouse aesthetic feelings in artists. Enchanted by the grace and elegance of the shapes and movements of birds, artists' artistic vocabulary includes compactness, vigour, strength, spontaneity, freshness, modesty, splendour, richness, elegance or ethereal beauty.

Furthermore, the proportions of birds' heads, necks, bodies and tails are close to the aesthetic golden rule. In other words, beauty is related to number and proportion. This also explains why in Chinese traditional paintings the legends and seals are arranged in exact proportion to the painting to achieve the best effect.

Another accomplished painter of birds was Xu Xi of the Song Dynasty. Emperor Taizong once said, "In my view, Xi is the only painter who creates vivid birds and flowers. I appreciate no other painter for such paintings." The author of the *Xuanhe Album of Paintings* wrote, "Huang Quan's paintings are lifelike but lack spirit, whereas Zhao Chang's paintings have spirit but do not look like real life. Only Xi possesses the merits of both." There were quite a number of painters of birds and flowers during the late Northern Song Dynasty, such as Ai Xuan, Wang Xiao, Zhao Jie, Ma Ben, Dai Wuan and Han Ruozhuo.

Zhao Jie was an emperor (Emperor Hui Zong) and he was good at both painting and calligraphy. His painting "Auspicious Cranes" shows only the ridge of the roof of his imperial hall at the bottom of the picture, leaving much space above for a flock of red-crowned cranes flying against the sky. The cranes convey a vivid rhythm, but from the ornithological point of view, the painting was not true to life, for in the painting the cranes' necks are bent during flight, but in actual life cranes fly with stretched necks. This shows the emperor-painter did not see cranes fly outside his palace.

Aside from the meticulously executed fine-brush paintings of birds and flowers at the time, another school of painters preferred to paint with bold strokes. This school developed conspicuously later. By the time of the Qing Dynasty (1644-1911) quite a number of outstanding painters of the freehand brushwork school, such as Bada Shanren, Shi Tao and Ren Bonian, had emerged. Ren Bonian, in particular, left a great many paintings of birds and flowers.

People get aesthetic and pleasant feelings from the singing of birds and the fragrance of flowers. The singing of birds first of all indicates the birds' territory. It also displays the charm of the male bird. Birds sing countless different melodies. The singing of larks and hwameis during breeding time is especially pleasant to the ear. The Chinese folk music "A Hundred Birds Paying Respect to the Phoenix" depicts the melodies of dozens of different birds and conveys the liveliness of nature.

The dancelike movements of birds have also drawn the attention of man since ancient times. Like human beings who convey their feelings through dance, birds make gestures and movements to convey their feelings. Chinese classics such as *Yi Jing* (the *Book of Changes*) and *Shang Shu* (the *Book of History*) mention dances that imitate the movements of birds.

In his constant contact with birds man began to appreciate the beautiful movements and singing of birds and the brilliance of their plumage. He began to create bird dances with gorgeous feathers as ornaments. Some bronze articles unearthed from Shizhai Mountain in Jinning County, beside Lake Dianchi in Yunnan Province, bear images of dancing girls with egret feathers on their heads imitating the movements of egrets. It is mentioned in *Tong Dian* (*A Comprehensive Study of History*) of the Tang Dynasty, "Birds reared in the palace" mimic the words "Long life!". It says that Empress Wu Zetian ordered a dance to be choreographed. The dance was performed by three dancers wearing wide-sleeved scarlet robes and feather headdresses depicting the flying of egrets. People of Korean nationality, living in northeast China, have crane dances that convey their love for cranes, often mentioned in their folklore as a symbol of happiness and an omen of a bumper harvest.

Shan Hai Jing (*Classic of Mountains and Seas*) records that "peafowls abound in the south . . . feathers in colourful patterns . . . start dancing at the clapping of hands." *Yi Wu Zhi* (*Records of Strange Things*) mentions that because people love the gorgeous plumage and graceful dance of peafowls, they learn to perform the peacock dance.

In south China people of various nationalities have a great love for birds. The people of the Miao, Yao, Dai, Yi, Wa, Gaoshan, Hani and Jingpo nationalities all have folk dances imitating the movements of birds. For example, the Dais have their peacock and woodpecker dances; the Bais have their crane and cormorant dances; the Naxis have their skylark dance; the Lahus have their quail and hwamei dances; the Lisus have their dove dance; the Hanis have their silver pheasant dance, and Tibetans have their golden sparrow dance. These dances either pay respects to heroes in history or express the dancers' aspirations and feelings. The quail dance of the Lahu nationality praises the fine qualities of the quail. The crane dance of the Bai nationality relates a tale in which two cranes helped the ancestors of the Bai people open up the jungles of the Cang Mountains beside Lake Erhai. The hwamei dance expresses people's longing for the arrival of spring. The peacock dance expresses people's hope for a peaceful life. The crane dance symbolizes favourable weather and good harvest. People in ancient times performed dances to worship spirits. Some tribes even took certain birds as their ancestors, named their tribes after birds or put up totems of bird images. Other bird dances, such as the humorous hwamei dance, just gave people a chance for merrymaking.

Birds are also closely connected with gardens and parks in China, where they have been reared since ancient times.

Among the ten scenic spots around the West Lake at Hangzhou there is a place called Orioles Singing amid Weeping Willows, and in the Summer Palace in Beijing the Listening to Orioles Pavilion is a beautiful spot to visitors.

A wonderful tourist attraction in Yunnan Province is the Stone Forest, where nature has carved the limestone rocks into a stone forest of grotesque shapes. Local people have named some of the strangely shaped stones after birds, such as Phoenix Combing Its Wings and Bird on a Cloud Terrace. Poets in the past wrote many poems praising the stone forest and its birds.

The beautiful gardens built in past dynasties in Suzhou, Jiangsu Province, have won world acclaim not only for their elegant architecture in traditional Chinese style but also for the many poetic names of the pavilions, halls, towers and terraces, which are linked with lovely birds, such as the Crane Kiosk, Phoenix Terrace and Mandarin Duck Pavilion.

The East Lake in Wuhan, Hubei Province, is attractive for its natural beauty. The green waters are graced by wild geese and ducks. Not far from the lake is the Yellow Crane Tower, which is said to have earned its present name after a fairy left there on the wings of a crane.

Bird feathers have been used by ladies in the West as ornaments. In feudal Chinese courts, however, the feathers of some birds were used to denote the different official ranks. Emperor Wudi of the Han Dynasty was the first to order his generals to wear the plumes of brown eared pheasants. In the Qing Dynasty low-ranking officials wore plumes of brown eared pheasants and high-ranking officials wore peacock feathers. The more "eyes" on the peacock feather the higher the rank. The brown eared pheasant is native to China and is known for its bellicocity. Feudal rulers wanted their generals to be as brave as the brown eared pheasant.

Chapter Six

Field Knowledge of Birds

A great variety of birds are found in China, thanks to the extremely diverse natural conditions of the country, which stretches across the frigid, temperate and tropical zones and is endowed with forests, grasslands, fertile fields and deserts, mountains towering 8,000 metres above sea level, highlands 5,000 metres above sea level and basins more than 100 metres below sea level.

To help us distinguish birds in the field, we use the following criteria: plumage, call, morphology, behaviour.

1. Feathers. The plumage of birds is easiest to distinguish. Birds can be devided into the following categories according to the colour of their feathers:

(1) Birds whose feathers are mainly black:
cormorant
black-crowned night-heron
black stork
moorhen
coot
David's laughing thrush
Indian jungle nightjar
white-rumped swift
house swallow
black drongo
crow
dipper
black bushchat
crested myna

brambling
masked hawfinch

(2) Birds with black and white feathers:
jacana
oyster catcher
pied woodpecker
pied kingfisher
magpie
jackdaw
collared crow
great tit
little forktail
magpie robin
chested myna
wagtail

(3) Birds whose feathers are mainly white:
swan
little egret
white stork
siberian crane
gull
swallow gull
paradise flycatcher (old male)

(4) Birds whose feathers are mainly grey:
black-crowned night heron
grey crane
blue hill pigeon
ashy minivet
ashy drongo
nuthatch
grey shrike
starling
masked hawfinch

(5) Birds whose feathers are mainly brown:
    bean goose
    eagle
    common quail
    rail
    plover
    owl
    lark
    grey tree pie
    hwamei
    wren
    straited mannikin
    house sparrow
    hawfinsh
    bunting
(6) Birds whose feathers are mainly green:
    thick-billed pigeon
    red-breasted parakeet
    barbet
    green woodpecker
    white-headed bulbul
    willow warbler
    flowerpecker
    silver eye
    greenfinch
(7) Birds whose feathers are mainly red or
    light brown:
    Chinese pond heron
    pheasant
    rail
    sandpiper
    hoopoe
    scarlet minivet (male)
    red-headed crowtit
    rubythroat
    red-tailed shrike
    rosefinch
    red crossbill
    brambling
(8) Birds whose feathers are mainly yellow:
    cattle egret
    yellow bittern
    scarlet minivet (female)
    oriole
    yellow-billed tit
    yellow-vented bulbul

yellow-breasted bunting
flycatcher
yellow wagtail
(9) Birds whose feathers are mainly blue:
    broad-billed roller
    black-capped kingfisher
    pitta
    long-tailed blue magpie
    bluethroat
    blue-and-white flycatcher

2. Cries: It is a convenient way to distinguish birds in the fields by listening to their cries or singing because usually birds are timid and like to hide themselves in the woods, thus making observation by the eye difficult.

(1) Those singing more or less methodically with a start, continuation and drawl:

a) With virtually a single whistling (such as the rosefinch, willow warbler, little bunting, tree creeper, etc.)

b) With a tremolo (such as the common bunting, brambling, oriole, wagtail, etc.)

c) With each cry consisting of two parts (the pipit, etc.)

(2) Those singing continuously without an obvious beginning and an ending:

a) Whistling without tremolo or cry (the wren, skylark, etc.)

b) Chirpping or tremor, voice very low (grey thrush, Siberian ground thrush, etc.)

c) Quick, short cries louder and more complicated than chirpping (such as the greenfinch)

(3) Each cry consists of short notes and there is a marked pause between two cries, or cries of different patterns change alternately with short pauses (the cuckoo, robin, etc.)

(4) Mimicking other birds (such as the hwamei, crested myna, grackle and parrot)

3. Morphological features: The morphological features of birds can help

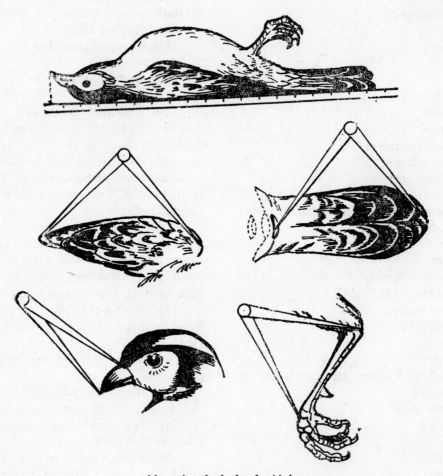

Measuring the body of a bird

us recognize birds in the fields. Take the form of the beak for example. Those with long bills are the crane, stork or egret family; those with big bills are the pelican, hornbill, etc; those with downward hooked bills are the crested ibis, etc. and those with bills crooked upward are the Avocet, sandpipers.

4.   Birds can also be told apart by their different behaviour. Take their flight for instance. Some fly in a straight line such as the ducks, some can glide for a long time such as the birds of prey, some fly in a wave-like pattern such as the wagtail family and the sparrows and some fly very fast and often change directions such as the house swallow and the swift. Similarly birds walk and rest in different manners.

Appendix 1 Morphology and Measurements of Birds

Outer features of a bird

1. **Head**: upper: (from front to rear): forehead, crown, occiput;

   side: lore, circumorbital, cheek, auricular;

   lower: chin

2. **Neck**: upper: nape;

   side: side of neck;

   lower: throat including gula (upper throat) and jugulum;

3. **Trunk**: upper: back and rump (back includes upper and lower back);

   side: side of breast, flank;

   lower: breast (including upper and lower breast), belly, crissum;

4. **Wing**; remiges: primaries, secondaries and tertiaries;

coverts: primaries, secondary coverts (greater, medium and lesser coverts);

alula (near the wing corner);

auxilaries (near the base of the wing);

5. Leg: thigh, shank, tarsometatarsus, toe, etc.

6. Tail: rectrice (including central and lateral rectrice), upper tail coverts, under tail coverts.

Measurements of birds used in classification:

1. Body length: from tip of bill to tip of tail

2. Bill length: shortest distance from the base of the bill, where feathers begin, to the tip of the upper beak

3. Wing length: from wing corner (carpal joint) to tip of longest flight feather

4. Tail length: from base of rectrice to tip of longest tail feather

5. Length of tarsometatarsus: from midpoint between tibia and tarsal joint to underside of lowest scale between tarsometatarsus and front of joint of middle toe.

In addition to the above, there are wingspread, gape length, claw length and such, which are measured when necessary.

---

1. body length
2. wingspread
3. wing length
4. tail length
5. beak length
6. beak length (minus cere)
7. length of gape
8. length of tarsometatarsus
9. length of claw

Measurements of the body of a bird

Appendix II Checklist of Birds in China

Order	Family	Genus	Species	Subspecies
1. Gaviiformes	1. Gaviidae	1	3	4
2. Podicipediformes	2. Podicipedidae	1	5	6
3. Procellariiformes	3. Diomedeidae	1	2	2
	4. Procellariidae	4	7	7
	5. Hydrobatidae	1	2	2
4. Pelecaniformes	6. Phaethontidae	1	3	3
	7. Pelecanidae	1	2	3
	8. Sulidae	1	2	2
	9. Phalacrocoracidae	1	5	5
	10. Fregatidae	1	3	4
5. Ciconiiformes	11. Ardeidae	10	20	26
	12. Ciconiidae	3	4	5
	13. Threskiornithidae	5	6	6
6. Anseriformes	14. Anatidae	19	46	51
7. Falconiformes	15. Accipitridae	22	46	73
	16. Falconidae	2	11	22
8. Galliformes	17. Tetraonidae	5	8	12
	18. Phasianidae	21	49	122

Order	Family	Genus	Species	Subspecies
9. Gruiformes	19. Turnicidae	1	3	4
	20. Gruidae	2	9	9
10. Charadriiformes	21. Rallidae	10	18	24
	22. Otididae	1	3	4
	23. Jacanidae	2	2	2
	24. Rostratulidae	1	1	1
	25. Haematopodidae	1	1	1
	26. Charadriidae	3	13	21
	27. Scolopacidae	14	38	43
	28. Recurvirostridae	3	3	3
	29. Phalaropodidae	1	2	2
	30. Burhinidae	1	1	1
	31. Glareolidae	1	2	2
11. Lariformes	32. Stercorariidae	1	1	1
	33. Laridae	10	32	39
	34. Rynchopidae	1	1	1
	35. Alcidae	3	3	3
12. Columbiformes	36. Pteroclididae	2	3	3
	37. Columbidae	8	31	51
13. Psittaciformes	38. Psittacidae	2	7	7
14. Cuculiformes	39. Cuculidae	7	17	25
15. Strigiformes	40. Tytonidae	2	3	5
	41. Strigidae	11	23	56

Order	Family	Genus	Species	Subspecies
16. Caprimulgiformes	42. Podargidae	1	1	1
	43. Caprimulgidae	2	7	12
17. Apodiformes	44. Apodidae	4	7	12
	45. Hemiprocnidae	1	1	1
18. Trogoniformes	46. Trogonidae	1	3	7
19. Coraciiformes	46. Alcedinidae	5	11	16
	47. Meropidae	2	6	7
	48. Coraciidae	2	3	3
	49. Upupidae	1	1	3
	50. Bucerotidae	4	4	4
20. Piciformes	51. Capitonidae	1	8	14
	52. Picidae	12	29	88
21. Passeriformes	1. Eurylaimidae	2	2	4
	2. Pittidae	2	7	11
	3. Alaudidae	6	12	40
	4. Hirundinidae	4	10	25
	5. Motacillidae	3	15	41
	6. Campephagidae	4	10	25
	7. Pycnonotidae	4	20	44
	8. Irenidae	3	6	8
	9. Bombycillidae	1	2	2
	10. Laniidae	1	9	27

Order	Family	Genus	Spe-cies	Sub-spe-cies
	11. Oriolidae	1	5	9
	12. Dicruridae	1	7	15
	13. Sturnidae	4	18	22
	14. Artamidae	1	1	1
	15. Corvidae	11	28	64
	16. Cinclidae	1	2	6
	17. Troglodytidae	1	1	7
	18. Prunellidae	1	9	18
	19. Muscicapidae			
	(1) Turdinae	18	80	125
	(2) Timaliinae	28	130	287
	(3) Sylviinae	19	85	150
	(4) Muscicapinae	8	39	55
	20. Paridae	4	21	17
	21. Sittidae	2	10	55
	22. Certhiidae	1	4	9
	23. Remizidae	2	2	4
	24. Dicaeidae	1	6	10
	25. Nectariniidae	4	12	19
	26. Zosteropidae	1	3	5
	27. Ploceidae	7	20	42
	28. Fringillidae	22	85	154

中 国 珍 禽

作者 许维枢

绘图 王玢莹

*

外文出版社出版

（中国北京百万庄路24号）

外文印刷厂印刷

中国国际图书贸易总公司

（中国国际书店）发行

北京399信箱

1989年（16开）第一版

（英）

ISBN 7-119-00069-1/K·10（外）

01715

13—E—1834 P